Your Happy Healthy Pet™

Saltwater Aquarium

2nd Edition

Gregory Skomal, PhD

Howell
Book House™

About the Author

Gregory Skomal is an accomplished marine biologist, underwater explorer, photographer, aquarist, and author. He has been a fisheries biologist with the Massachusetts Division of Marine Fisheries since 1987 and currently heads up the Massachusetts Shark Research Program. He has written numerous scientific research papers and has appeared in a number of film and television shark documentaries, including programs for National Geographic, Discovery Channel, and ESPN.

Although his research passion for the last twenty years has been sharks, he is also an avid aquarist and has written eight books on aquarium keeping. His home and laboratory are on the island of Martha's Vineyard off the coast of Massachusetts.

About Howell Book House

Since 1961, Howell Book House has been America's premier publisher of pet books. We're dedicated to companion animals and the people who love them, and our books reflect that commitment. Our stable of authors—training experts, veterinarians, breeders, and other authorities—is second to none. And we've won more Maxwell Awards from the Dog Writers Association of America than any other publisher.

As we head toward the half-century mark, we're more committed than ever to providing new and innovative books, along with the classics our readers have grown to love. This year, we're launching several exciting new initiatives, including redesigning the Howell Book House logo and revamping our biggest pet series, Your Happy Healthy Pet™, with bold new covers and updated content. From bringing home a new puppy to competing in advanced equestrian events, Howell has the titles that keep animal lovers coming back again and again.

Contents

Shopping List

You'll need to do a bit of stocking up before you bring your fish home. Below is a basic list of some must-have supplies. For more detailed information on the selection of each item below, consult chapter 2. For specific guidance on what fish food you'll need, review chapter 6.

☐ Tank   ☐ Hydrometer

☐ Aquarium stand   ☐ Tank decorations

☐ Tank Hood   ☐ Gravel

☐ Filters   ☐ Live rock (optional)

☐ Protein skimmer   ☐ Algae scraper

☐ Water-quality test kits   ☐ Aquarium vacuum

☐ Air pump/airstones   ☐ Fishnet

☐ Powerhead (optional)   ☐ 5-gallon bucket

☐ Aquarium light   ☐ Siphon hose

☐ Heater   ☐ Fish food

☐ Thermometer

There are likely to be a few other items that you're dying to pick up before bringing your fish home. Use the following blanks to note any additional items you'll be shopping for.

☐ _____

☐ _____

☐ _____

☐ _____

☐ _____

☐ _____

☐ _____

Pet Sitter's Guide

We can be reached at (___)_____-_____ Cellphone (___)_____-_____

_____

We will return on _____ (date) at _____ (approximate time)

Other individual to contact in case of emergency: _____

_____

Fish species: _____

_____

_____

_____

Care Instructions

In the following blank lines, let the sitter know what to feed, how much, and when; what tasks need to be performed daily; and what weekly tasks they'll be responsible for.

Morning _____

_____

_____

_____

_____

Evening _____

_____

_____

_____

Other tasks and special instructions _____

_____

_____

_____

_____

_____

_____

Part I

All About Marine Aquariums

The Saltwater Fish

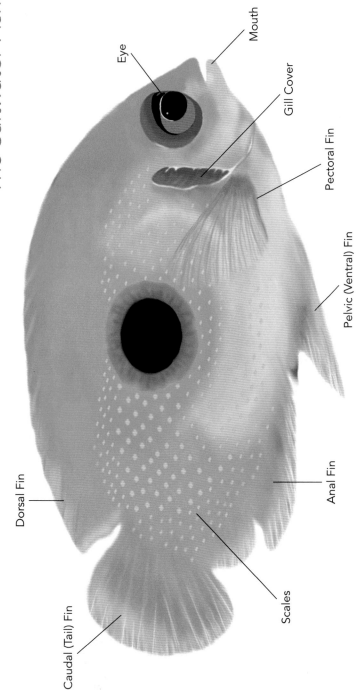

Mouth

Eye

Gill Cover

Pectoral Fin

Pelvic (Ventral) Fin

Dorsal Fin

Anal Fin

Caudal (Tail) Fin

Scales

Chapter 1

Marine Fish Basics

If you are interested in keeping a saltwater aquarium, this is the book for you. Perhaps you've had a freshwater tank and would like to graduate to the more complex marine environment. Perhaps, like me, you are a fish enthusiast. The world of fish is both fascinating and complex. This book will help you to understand that world and will teach you what you need to know to set up and maintain a successful saltwater aquarium. To do that, you'll need a general knowledge of fish, their anatomy and biology. You'll also need a thorough understanding of their proper care and husbandry.

First, we will take a look at fish anatomy and what makes these animals so unique. There are no fewer than 12,000 kinds of saltwater fishes, so it is difficult to describe the "typical" fish. For the most part, however, all fish have some common attributes.

Then we'll examine the aquarium and the importance of meeting the biological needs of fish. As we do, I'll describe the critical differences between freshwater and saltwater aquariums. We'll walk through the basics of aquarium setup and proper maintenance. We'll cover proper nutrition and feeding, fish health and disease, and I'll tell you about some advanced marine aquarium techniques.

The only topic we will not discuss is saltwater fish breeding; so few have been successfully spawned in captivity that this is clearly an endeavor best left to the experts.

Aquarium Fish

The group of aquatic animals we call fish has evolved for more than 400 million years to be the most numerous and diverse of the major vertebrate groups (animals with backbones). Fish live in all the waters of the world, adapting with an incredible variety of forms, lifestyles, and behaviors. From the seasonal freshwater stream, desert spring, and salty bay to the coral reef, open ocean, and deep abyss, fish have found suitable niches. There are well over 20,000 species of fishes that currently inhabit Earth, and many more are being discovered every year.

Salt water covers more than 70 percent of Earth's surface and freshwater only 1 percent, so you would expect that there would be many more marine (saltwater) species than freshwater species of fish. Surprisingly, only 58 percent of the world's fish species live exclusively in salt water. Of these, only about 13 percent are generally found in the open ocean. By far, the majority of marine species live in the narrow band of water less than 500 feet deep along the coastlines of land masses.

As you move into the warm waters of the tropics, fish species diversify and the number of species dramatically increases. Fishes that inhabit the warm waters of the coral reef are usually the most sought after for aquariums because of their incredible beauty. This book will address the characteristics, requirements, and husbandry of these creatures.

Saltwater vs. Freshwater Fishes

The fundamental differences between freshwater and saltwater fish are directly linked to the two environmental extremes in which they live. In general, freshwater fishes are hardier than their marine counterparts, having evolved to withstand the rapid and dramatic changes in water conditions that occur inland. Most marine species have adapted to more or less constant environmental conditions; they have not evolved the adaptive mechanisms to deal with sudden environmental changes, such as those that may occur in the home aquarium. This, of course, makes saltwater fishes more difficult to keep in captivity.

Obviously, salt water contains much higher concentrations of salt (sodium chloride) than fresh water. In addition, many other dissolved elements are present in higher concentrations in salt water than they are in fresh water. These minerals together are called "salts," and the proportion of dissolved salts in water is referred to as its salinity or specific gravity.

Now, a fish is surrounded by the chemistry of the water it lives in. That fish has water and dissolved salts in its body as well. A fish surrounded by fresh water has more salts in its body than there are in the surrounding water, and a fish surrounded by salt water has less salts in its body than there are in the surrounding water. Both these situations can create real problems for the fish, because a process called osmosis causes water to flow through cell membranes from areas of low salinity to areas of high salinity. This means that the fish in fresh water is

All saltwater animals, including this starfish, are specially adapted to be able to regulate the amount of salts in their bodies.

constantly subjected to an influx of water and the marine fish is always threatened by the loss of water. Although anatomically the two groups of fishes are similar in appearance, they have evolved two very different ways of living in these chemically different environments.

Osmoregulation

The process of maintaining water balance in the body is called osmoregulation. You need to understand the basic principles of osmoregulation because it has important implications for fish in captivity. To start with, it explains why freshwater fish cannot be kept in salt water (and vice versa)—because their bodies cannot adapt to the change.

As a way of maintaining their internal salinity, freshwater fish drink very little water and produce large quantities of dilute urine. By contrast, most marine fish drink large quantities of water and eliminate salts in small amounts of highly concentrated urine and feces, as well as at the gills. So the kidneys of these two groups are very different. (Sharks and their close relatives, the rays, are exceptions to this pattern in marine fish. These species concentrate urea in their tissues and blood to offset the loss of water.)

In addition, since marine fish must expend a lot of energy to prevent the loss of water and excrete salt, they require good health and lots of food. Also, marine fish drink large amounts of water, so the quality of the water must be very good. Finally, abrupt changes in salinity will disturb the internal chemistry of marine fish. For these reasons, marine fishkeeping can be more difficult than maintaining a freshwater system. But with a little extra effort, it can be infinitely rewarding.

Fish Anatomy

Despite their differences in osmoregulation, freshwater and marine fish have many similarities. Since water is 800 times denser than air, fish have developed a variety of ways to move easily, breathe, and feed in a dense medium. Let's take a closer look at the unique adaptations that have enabled fish to live so successfully in the water. Anatomical adaptations include body shape, fins, scales, and swim bladder.

Body Shape

A great deal can be learned about a fish by looking at its body form or shape. Fish that are streamlined or bullet shaped are specially adapted to open waters, while flat or stocky fish are well adapted for living on or close to the bottom.

Fins

Almost all species of fish have fins in one form or another. The fins are critically important appendages that enable the fish to propel and stabilize itself, maneuver, and stop. In some cases, fins protect the fish as well. The fins have many shapes and functions, depending on the type of fish and the habitat it lives in. Bottom-dwelling, sedentary, or slower-moving fish have rounded fins, while faster, open-water fish generally have longer, pointed fins.

Fins can be either paired (one on each side of the fish) or unpaired. The pectoral fins are the forwardmost paired fins, and are located on each side just behind or below the gills. They help the fish stabilize itself, turn, maneuver, hover, and swim backward.

The pelvic fins are also paired and vary the most in position. In some fish, the pelvics lie under the fish toward the rear. In others, including many tropical fish, the pelvics are closer to the head, just below the pectorals. The pelvic fins act as brakes and also aid in stabilizing and turning the fish.

The dorsal and anal fins are unpaired fins that protrude from the top and bottom of the fish, respectively. Dorsal fins may be elongated or short, elaborate

The Basics of Fish Anatomy

There are thousands of species of fishes, all uniquely adapted to their particular environments. However, most share fundamental characteristics that enable them to be classified together as fish.

Gills: These enable the fish to take in oxygen from the water.

Fins: These move the fish through the water, providing propulsion and steering.

Swim bladder: This organ fills up with or releases air, thereby controlling the fish's level in the water column.

Lateral line: This sensory organ alerts the fish to movement close by and helps schooling fish move in synchrony.

Scales: These streamline and protect the body of the fish as it moves through the water.

or simple, singular or multiple. Some species of fish completely lack a dorsal or anal fin. Both fins help stabilize the fish and keep it moving straight.

The caudal or tail fin is an unpaired fin that is largely responsible for propelling the fish forward. This fin is the source of forward momentum for most fish and can also assist in turning and braking. The shape of the tail can tell you a lot about the lifestyle of a fish. Faster fish have deeply forked caudal fins, while many deep-bodied fishes and bottom-dwellers have square or rounded tails.

In general, the main supporting structures of fish fins are soft rays. However, anyone who has handled a fish knows that the dorsal, anal, or pectoral fins of many species also have spines. These sharp, bony structures provide protection against predators (and people who try to pick the fish up).

Scales

The bodies of most fish are covered in scales. The scales are made of a hard, bony substance and protect the fish, reducing the chance of injuries and infections. Covering the scales is a very thin layer of epidermal tissue that contains

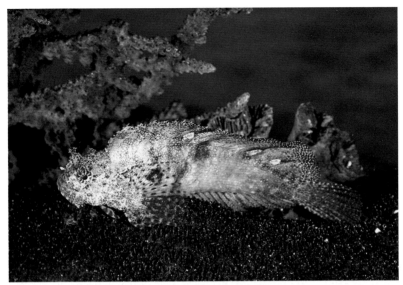

Fins come in a wide variety of shapes and sizes. This is a Jeweled Blenny.

mucous cells. These cells produce the slimy texture we normally attribute to fish. The mucous coating not only protects the fish against injury and infection, but also helps the fish move more easily through the water, reducing friction between the body and the surrounding water.

Fish scales are translucent and lack color. The vibrant colors of tropical fish come from specialized pigment cells called chromatophores, which lie in the deeper dermal layer of the skin. The color of the fish depends on the types of chromatophores present. Fish that are clear, like the freshwater Glassfish, lack these pigments.

The bodies of sharks and rays are not covered with scales, but with tiny scale-like teeth called denticles. They feel like sandpaper and serve the same role as scales do in other fish.

Swim Bladder

Living in the dense medium of water presents a few problems for fish; one of these is buoyancy. Maintaining a certain level in the water column without having to work too hard is very important to fish. To accomplish this, most species have a special organ called a swim bladder. This gas-filled sac, located in the abdominal cavity, acts as a life vest, keeping the fish wherever it wants to be in the water column. There are many types of swim bladders, ranging from the simple single-chambered sac of the trout to the three-chambered bladder of the codfish. Some fish have a direct connection between the esophagus and the swim bladder, so they simply have to swallow air to fill it. Others must rely on gas exchange from specialized blood vessels in the circulatory system.

In addition to its role in buoyancy, the swim bladder helps to mechanically amplify sound for better hearing in certain species of fish.

However, not all species of marine fish have swim bladders. For example, sharks have large fatty livers instead of swim bladders to help maintain buoyancy. Their skeletons are composed of cartilage, which also reduces their density in water. Many species of tuna also lack swim bladders; their streamlined bodies and forward speed help them maintain their level in the water column.

Mouth and Digestion

Just as the body shape of a fish can tell you a lot about its swimming habits, the mouth can tell you something about how it eats. Generally, bottom feeders have mouths that point downward, while surface feeders have mouths that point up. The size of the mouth is usually directly related to the size of the fish's preferred food. For example, large predators like Sharks and Barracuda have large mouths armed with teeth for consuming other fish. Fish like the Butterflyfish, which normally feeds on small aquatic invertebrates, have smaller mouths.

Some tropical marine fish have specialized mouths for specific feeding strategies. The sharp "beak" of the Parrotfish is helpful for feeding on the coral reef. The Basking Shark, which feeds on microscopic plankton, has a mouth that opens very wide and specialized gill rakers that enable it to sift the water.

The shape of a fish's mouth gives you a clue about what and how it eats. This is a Longnose Hawkfish.

Marine fish have a relatively straightforward digestive system, which varies from species to species. In general, food passes from the mouth and down the esophagus, where it is digested in the stomach and intestines; waste is excreted out the anus. However, some species of fish lack stomachs and have elongated, supercoiled intestines. Others, like Parrotfish, have specialized grinding teeth in their pharynx that are used to grind food. Again, the Sharks and Rays are different in that they have a specialized large intestine called the spiral valve.

Breathing

Like land animals, fish need oxygen to live. However, instead of lungs, fish have specialized organs called gills, which enable them to extract oxygen from the water. The gills of a fish act like our lungs; they provide oxygen to the fish's blood and remove carbon dioxide. This oxygen is then transported by the blood to the tissues of the fish, where it is used to produce energy. Water contains much less oxygen than air, and fish must breathe ten to thirty times more water to get the same amount of oxygen that a land animal would get from air.

Most fish have four gills on each side of the head. The branchial chamber, which holds the gills, is protected by a single gill flap, or operculum. In contrast, Sharks and their relatives possess five to seven gills, each with its own gill slit.

To breathe, the fish pulls water into the mouth and pushes it into the branchial chamber over the gills and out the operculum. As water passes over the membranes and filaments of the gills, oxygen and carbon dioxide are exchanged between the water and the blood. To accomplish this, the gills have a very high number of blood vessels, which carry oxygen to the rest of the fish.

Other Organs

Aside from the notable exceptions outlined above, fish typically possess the general circulatory, digestive, respiratory, and nervous system features that are common to most vertebrates. If you are curious to learn more about these systems, examine the bibliography in the appendix for books that will give you more detailed descriptions of the unique anatomy of fish.

Senses

With few exceptions, fish have five senses that they use to feed, avoid predators, communicate, and reproduce.

Sight

The eyes of most fishes are similar to our own, except they lack eyelids and their irises work much more slowly. Some species of Sharks, however, have specialized upside-down eyelids called nictitating membranes, which protect the eyes. The location of the spherical lenses of fish eyes renders most fish nearsighted. Although it varies from species to species, it is generally thought that fish can detect color.

When it comes to keeping fish in captivity, the aquarist should remember that rapid changes in light intensity can shock a fish. Gradual changes in light enable the fish to accommodate and avoid temporary blindness.

Rapid changes in light intensity can shock a fish. Your fish prefer gradual changes in light. This is a Popeye Catalufa.

Hearing

Water is a much more efficient conductor of sound than air. Therefore, sound carries much farther and faster in water. Fish do not have external ears, but they do have an inner ear that is not noticeable on the outside of the fish. The auditory component of the inner ear consists of the sacculus and the lagena, which house the sensory components of hearing, the otoliths. Sound vibrations pass through the water, through the fish's body, and reverberate off the otoliths in the inner ear. As mentioned previously, in some cases the swim bladder articulates with the ear to amplify sound.

Smell

Fish have external nostrils called nares, which draw water into and out of the olfactory organ located above the mouth and below the eyes. Water flows through the nares and into the olfactory pits, where odors are perceived and communicated to the brain via a large nerve. The olfactory system of the fish is not attached to the respiratory system, as it is in humans, but remains isolated from the mouth and gills. Smell is particularly important to fishes in detecting prey and mates.

Fish have a special sense organ along their sides called the lateral line system, which roughly corresponds with the stripe on this Yellowhead Wrasse.

Taste

This is generally a close-range sense in fishes and is especially helpful in identifying both food and noxious substances. While our taste buds are only found in our mouths, fish also have taste buds on the external surfaces of the skin, lips, and fins. Catfish have special barbels (their "whiskers") that are packed with taste buds and help the fish to detect food items in murky waters.

Touch

Fish have a very specialized organ called the lateral line system, which helps them to detect water movements. Sensory receptors lying along the surface of the fish's body in low pits or grooves detect water displacement and, therefore, give the fish the sensation of touch.

The lateral line is easily visible along the sides of most fish. This unique system helps the fish to detect other fishes, sense water movement and currents, avoid obstacles, and swim in schools. In addition to the lateral line system, Sharks and Rays possess sophisticated sensory organs called the ampullae of Lorenzini, which are capable of detecting weak electrical fields.

Chapter 2

The Saltwater Aquarium

I t is no surprise that humans have enjoyed keeping fish in aquariums for centuries. The common Goldfish was kept in captivity in China as long ago as the year 265. Care and husbandry of fish has come a long way over the centuries.

There was a time when virtually all of the tropical fish kept in captivity were taken from their native homes. This practice, if not conducted wisely, contributes to the degradation of tropical habitats and the local depletion of species. While modern husbandry techniques have taken pressure off natural stocks and many aquarium species are now bred in captivity, these are largely freshwater species.

Although they represent only a fraction of the total number of ornamental fishes sold, most saltwater species are still harvested from the wild. The most popular of these fishes come primarily from coral reef ecosystems. If managed properly, the coral reefs around the world can be harvested without harm. Coral reefs are extremely productive because of their size and the competitive nature of the inhabitants. Care should be taken, however, not to purchase fish that may have been harvested in areas that do not practice the sound conservation of natural reefs. Stay informed using the sources listed in the appendix, and make it a point to ask your dealer about where they get their fishes. Fish in their natural environment are subjected to many challenges to their survival. Most of these involve natural processes of predation, feeding, reproduction, and disease. Natural catastrophic events that alter water quality are rare, and fish can generally avoid them by moving to other areas. In many ways, fish in the wild are very much responsible for themselves. (A possible exception to this involves fish living in areas assaulted by pollution.)

Meeting the Needs of Your Fish

Fish maintained in the artificial environment of an aquarium are also faced with survival challenges. Most of these challenges cannot be met by the fish and must be met by the fishkeeper. That's you. When you take it upon yourself to set up an aquarium, you are accepting the responsibility of meeting all of the needs of its inhabitants. This includes maintaining high water quality, proper feeding, correct water temperature, a balanced fish community of the proper density, appropriate habitat and shelter, and sufficient lighting. The fish are totally dependent upon you. If they get sick or diseased, you must treat them.

As you gain experience as an aquarist, you may go beyond the basics and breed your fish or establish specialty tanks. But it's important to start slowly and develop your talents. If you are an experienced freshwater aquarist, you will learn that marine fish are less tolerant of less-than-optimal water quality conditions, and you must be meticulous in your care. Be sure to keep records of all your experiences, so you can learn from your mistakes.

Before you buy your aquarium supplies and fish, try to visit all the local aquarium stores so you can choose one or two to work with. If you have worked successfully with a freshwater aquarium dealer, this is the logical place to start with your marine interests. It's very important to establish a good working

Begin by finding a dealer who can give you good advice about your saltwater aquarium and has healthy stock. This is a Flame Scallop.

relationship with a dealer because you may need someone to go to for advice on the setup and maintenance of your aquarium.

You want someone who maintains a good, clean business, has healthy fish in the store, and is always willing to answer your questions. The good dealer gives you invaluable information about new and reliable products. They want to help you to maintain your system correctly. Try to avoid dealers who do not take the time to explain things to you. I've always preferred shops that cater to the needs of aquarists at all levels, are willing to special-order supplies, and would rather send you elsewhere than sell you an improper choice.

When you settle on one or two dealers, you are ready to begin planning your aquarium.

The Tank

Before you choose your aquarium setup, take the time to plan every aspect of its use. Determine beforehand where you are going to set the aquarium. To avoid excessive growth of algae, avoid placing the aquarium in direct sunlight. Choose a location that has an adequate electrical supply and is not too far from a source of water.

Make sure the structure of your building will hold the full aquarium. Water weighs about 8.4 pounds per gallon, so a 30-gallon tank weighs 250 pounds, not including gravel and other furnishings.

> **TIP**
>
> Think carefully about where the tank will be placed because once the aquarium is set up, it cannot easily be moved.

While well-used living areas can provide excellent settings for aquariums, too much activity tends to spook the fish into hiding. Keeping the aquarium in a rarely used area also tends to make fish skittish when people approach.

Finally, choose a location that can tolerate a water spill. Even the most meticulous aquarists spill water around an aquarium, and in many cases water will splash from a tank.

Tank Size

The general rule is to buy the largest tank you can afford and accommodate in your home. The reason for this is fairly straightforward: Fish require adequate space to swim and sufficient oxygen to live; both are determined by the size of the tank. The oxygen content of water is related to the surface area of the tank and the temperature of the water. Warmer water has less oxygen than colder water. Since most marine tropical fish prefer water warmer than 75 degrees Fahrenheit, the amount of oxygen may be limited in the tank. If a tank has a lot of surface area, which is dictated by its length and width, then it has more room for gas exchange at the surface. This means more oxygen entering the water and more toxic gases leaving the water. Hence, larger tanks can hold more fish.

As you consider the size of your aquarium, think about the number of fish you would like to keep. Most aquarists use fish length and tank volume to estimate the number of fish that a marine aquarium can hold. Larger fish consume more oxygen and therefore require more aquarium space. The general rule is 1 inch (2.5 cm) of fish per 4 gallons (18 liters) of water for the first six months. After this initial period, you can gradually increase fish density to 1 inch per 2 gallons (9 liters) of water. For example, a 40-gallon aquarium should contain no more than 10 inches of fish for the first six months. These may be one 3-inch Queen Angel, two 1-inch Clownfish, one 2-inch Regal Tang, one 1-inch Bicolor Blenny, and two 1-inch Beau Gregories. After six months, additional fish may be added gradually to increase the total number of inches to 20.

Long tanks are much better than tall tanks because surface area is so important to the capacity and health of your aquarium. Even though both tanks may hold the same volume of water, an upright (tall) tank has a much lower carrying capacity of fish because of its smaller surface area. The minimum size starter tank for the saltwater aquarium should be 30 gallons.

Consider the size of your fish when you are stocking your aquarium. This Ocellated Damselfish will grow to be 4 inches long.

Tank Tips

Here are some basic things to keep in mind when choosing your aquarium tank.

- Choose the largest tank you can afford and accommodate.
- Choose a long, low tank rather than a tall one.
- Never use a Goldfish bowl.
- Choose a tank with no scratches.
- Make sure there are no gaps in the seams.

Once you've decided on the appropriate size of your aquarium, choosing the tank itself is fairly straightforward. For decades, home aquariums were made only of rectangular glass plates sealed with a silicone rubber cement. These were by far the most common and practical aquariums to buy and they are still quite common in the trade. They are built for the sole purpose of housing living animals and are, therefore, nontoxic. They don't easily scratch, either.

In recent years, acrylic aquariums have become very popular for a number of reasons. They are molded and have few seams, making them more transparent. Acrylic is also lighter than glass and is offered in more shapes and sizes than standard glass aquariums. It tends to be stronger than glass, so it will not crack or shatter as easily. However, acrylic tanks do scratch easily and they can be quite a bit more expensive. Algae scrapers and tank decorations will damage the tank when not properly handled.

Whether you choose glass or acrylic depends on your personal preference and your pocketbook. Regardless, make sure there are no scratches and that there are no gaps in any of the seams when you pick out your new tank.

The Aquarium Stand

The best support for the heavy weight of the aquarium and all its components is a commercially manufactured aquarium stand. This specialized piece of furniture is built to hold a full aquarium. Since salt water is very corrosive, a wooden stand tends to last longer than wrought iron.

Homemade stands and common household furniture may look sturdy, but they can fail under the heavy load. Stand failure can be costly to an aquarist and to a homeowner, so don't try to save money on your support for the aquarium.

If you decide not to buy a commercially built stand, cut a ⅝-inch sheet of plywood and a ½-inch sheet of polystyrene to the dimensions of the tank, and place both under the tank. These layers will even out any imperfections in the supporting surface and distribute the load.

The Tank Hood

An essential item for any aquarium is a hood (also called a canopy or cover). This important piece of equipment performs a variety of functions. First, it prevents unwanted items from entering the tank and injuring the fish. Second, it keeps overzealous fish from jumping out of the tank. (Remember, fish cannot breathe air, and nothing is worse than finding your pet on the floor next to the aquarium in the morning.) Third, the cover prevents water from splashing to the walls and floor, causing damage.

Fourth, it slows the rate of water evaporation from the tank. Water will condense on the cover and re-enter the tank instead of evaporating into the room.

An aquarium hood will help keep your fish and your water in the tank, where they belong. This is a Jeweled Tang.

This limits the necessity of adding more water. When water evaporates from a seawater aquarium, the salts do not leave the tank, but instead become more concentrated, thereby increasing the salinity of the water. This will disturb the fish and the water quality if it is not carefully monitored.

Fifth, the hood helps the aquarium retain heat, thereby reducing the use of the heater. And finally, the hood keeps water from damaging the aquarium light and prevents a potentially dangerous electrical problem.

The hood is generally fitted to the dimensions of the tank and can be adjusted to allow for aquarium accessories. Make sure it is made of thick glass or plastic so it can support the weight of other aquarium components, if necessary. Also, it should be segmented so the entire assembly need not be removed to feed the fish or work in the tank.

For the beginner, I strongly recommend the type of hood that also houses the aquarium light. These units are self-contained and designed to keep water away from the lighting unit. I've always felt that the tank, stand, and hood should be built by the same manufacturer and purchased as a package. This ensures the aquarium components are not mismatched, and it also may be less expensive.

The Water

The most important requirement of healthy fish is clean water. Fish in the natural marine environment live in an open system where water quality is generally not a problem. Products of respiration and digestion are readily swept away and naturally filtered. The sheer volume of water keeps these substances at extremely low levels.

In contrast, fish housed in an aquarium live in a closed system where the products of respiration and digestion remain until they are removed. The primary piece of equipment that removes these toxic substances from the aquarium is the filter. Before we discuss filtration and the types of filters available to the aquarist, it is important to examine the attributes of water quality and the natural wastes of fish.

Sea Water

The chemical composition of sea water is consistent throughout the world. Although sea water is 96 percent pure water, it also contains many dissolved minerals. Eighty-five percent of the mineral content is sodium and chlorine, but magnesium, sulphate, calcium, and potassium amount to another 13 percent, and bicarbonate and sixty-eight other elements, in trace quantities, make up the remaining 2 percent.

> ## Water Quality
>
> Marine fish are accustomed to much more stable environmental conditions than their freshwater counterparts. They are very sensitive to even small amounts of toxins and, hence, are more difficult to keep in captivity. Therefore, maintaining excellent water quality is critical. This means monitoring and occasionally adjusting several water parameters, including temperature, pH, oxygen, salinity, and nitrogenous compounds.

The beginner may be inclined to use natural sea water for a home aquarium. However, for several reasons, I strongly recommend that you use one of the synthetic salt mixes that are available at your pet store. First, if you do not live in the tropics, your local sea water is cold water that contains species of plankton that are not adapted to tropical temperatures. Elevating the temperature causes these organisms to die or rapidly proliferate, yielding polluted and poor-quality water. Second, the logistics of traveling back and forth to the seashore for large quantities of water will ultimately render its use impractical. Third, there are no guarantees that your water source is free of pollution. Seemingly clean sea water may contain high levels of toxic compounds and metals. Why take chances?

The science of marine chemistry has yielded salt mixes that mimic sea water without the potential toxins. These mixes can be dissolved in ordinary tap water for the home aquarium. You should always mix up additional salt water for water changes and emergencies. Batches of salt water should be stored in nonmetallic containers in a cool, dark place until needed.

Salinity

Marine species of fish thrive in water that has a very specific level of dissolved salts. Therefore, the amount of dissolved salts, or salinity, in your aquarium water must be measured frequently and maintained at the level that is best for your fish. To directly measure salinity, you need equipment that can be expensive for the average aquarist. Therefore, the easiest and most practical way to measure the salinity in your tank is to measure specific gravity. Technically, specific gravity refers to the ratio of the density of sea water to the density of pure water at various temperatures. Pure water has a specific gravity of 1.000. Water with a specific gravity of 1.021 is 1.021 times denser than pure water.

Use a hydrometer to measure specific gravity in the aquarium. This is an essential piece of equipment for the marine aquarist, and it must be used every couple of days. You can get a floating tube–type hydrometer or a needle type, which is easier to read.

Specific gravity should be in the range of 1.021 and 1.024, but more important, it should be maintained at a very even level within this range. Even minor fluctuations can cause problems for your fish.

The major cause of salinity changes is evaporation from the tank. When water evaporates in a

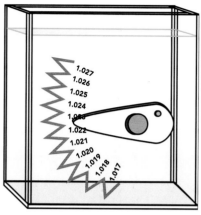

Check the salinity of the water by using a hydrometer to measure specific gravity. Even minor fluctuations can cause problems for your fish.

marine aquarium, the salts remain in solution and the water becomes more concentrated, thereby increasing the salinity and the specific gravity. You must constantly monitor water levels in the aquarium to prevent these fluctuations. Evaporation is easily remedied by adding fresh water to the tank—not additional salt water. Don't wait until levels have significantly dropped before you top off the tank. Instead, do so regularly with small quantities from the tap.

There can be some loss of salt from the tank due to crystallization on the hood and other fixtures and losses from the protein skimmer (see page 38). Keep an eye on the hydrometer, but be mindful that water evaporation occurs faster than salt loss.

pH

When we talk about pH, we are really referring to levels of hydrogen ions in solution. Ions are simply atoms with an electrical charge. We measure the number of hydrogen atoms on a pH scale. The pH scale tells us how many hydrogen atoms are in a solution and, therefore, how acidic it is. The lower the number on the scale, the more hydrogen atoms.

The pH scale ranges from 0 to 14; a pH of 7 is neutral, a pH of 1 is very acidic, and a pH of 14 is very alkaline. This scale is logarithmic, meaning that each number is 10 times stronger than the preceding number. For example, a pH of 2 is 10 times more acidic than a pH of 3 and 100 times more acidic than a pH of 4.

Salt water is more alkaline than fresh water. If you had a freshwater aquarium, you probably maintained the pH within the range of 6.5 to 7.5. By contrast, the

The Fishkeeper's Responsibilities

The fishkeeper (that's you) has an obligation to care for the fish he or she has brought home. Because the fish are contained in an artificial environment, it is up to you to establish and maintain their living space and keep it healthy and safe. You are responsible for providing:

- Excellent water quality
- Proper feeding
- Correct water temperature
- A balanced fish community of the proper density
- Appropriate habitat and shelter
- Sufficient lighting

Make sure you are ready to accept these responsibilities and the daily chores that go with them before you start shopping for your aquarium.

pH of sea water is about 8.2; a saltwater aquarium should be maintained between 8.1 and 8.3.

A number of factors influence the pH in your aquarium. These include the amount of carbon dioxide and fish wastes in the water. The accumulation of either or both of these will cause the water to become acidic and the pH to drop.

Make sure to add a pH test kit to your shopping list. It's very simple to use and is an important step in monitoring the quality of your aquarium water. Monitor the pH every week to detect any changes. An abrupt drop in pH may indicate an increase of carbon dioxide or nitrogenous fish wastes. An increase in aeration and a partial water change will be necessary to alleviate the problem before the lives of your fish are compromised.

The Nitrogen Cycle

Fish (and marine invertebrates) are living creatures that require food, which, with the help of oxygen that they obtain from the water, is broken down for energy and growth. These processes produce waste products that are returned to the environment through the gills and in the urine and feces. These wastes are primarily carbon dioxide and nitrogenous compounds such as ammonia, which are extremely toxic to fish.

In the aquarium, these wastes must be removed. Carbon dioxide generally leaves the water through aeration at the surface or as part of photosynthesis by algae in the aquarium. Ammonia must be converted to nitrite, which is then converted to nitrate, a less toxic compound. This process of ammonia conversion is called the nitrogen cycle.

The nitrogen cycle is driven by bacteria. Now, as we all know, there are good bacteria and bad bacteria. The good bacteria that convert ammonia (NH_4) into nitrite (NO_2) belong to the genus *Nitrosomonas*. Nitrite, in turn, is converted into nitrate (NO_3) by bacteria of the genus *Nitrobacter*. These processes are known collectively as nitrification.

> **CAUTION**
>
> Your marine animals are not the only source of nitrogenous wastes in your aquarium. Every time you feed your pets, excess food decomposes into harmful compounds, including ammonia. That's why it is important to feed your fish carefully, so they do not leave excess food uneaten in the aquarium.

What goes in will eventually come out. Fish wastes must be removed from the water, through filtering and a process called the nitrogen cycle. This is a Blue Devil Damselfish.

A healthy aquarium depends greatly on the nitrogen cycle to convert toxic ammonia into less toxic nitrogen compounds. This cycle can only be properly established in a biological filter, which is a requirement for all marine aquariums. Even with a properly working biological filter, the levels of ammonia, nitrite, and nitrate should be monitored frequently. This can be done with commercial test kits that are available at your aquarium supply store.

Types of Filters

In the aquarium system, nitrogen compounds are readily removed by the filtration system. There are three basic types of filtration: mechanical, chemical, and biological.

- **Mechanical filtration** physically removes suspended particles from the water by passing it through a fine filter medium. External power filters and canister filters provide rapid mechanical filtration.
- **Chemical filtration** involves chemically treating water to remove toxic substances. When you add activated carbon to an external power filter, you are providing chemical filtration.
- **Biological filtration** uses the nitrogen cycle to remove toxic compounds from the water. An example of a biological filter is the trickle or wet-dry filter that relies on established bacterial colonies to convert nitrogenous wastes to nitrate. Although this type of filtration requires some time to establish a working bacterial colony, it provides the best kind of filtration.

Most commercially manufactured aquarium filters provide all three kinds of filtration. However, you still must match the filter with the aquarium. How much you need to clean your water depends on the type of aquarium you plan to set up. Invertebrate and reef aquariums need to have the highest possible water quality for their inhabitants. Invertebrates such as corals, sponges, and anemones are very sensitive to even the smallest amounts of harmful substances like ammonia. A fish-only aquarium does not need to keep sensitive invertebrates alive, so the filtration system can be less efficient, and, perhaps, a little less expensive.

The size of the aquarium is important as well. It is very important to size your filtration system to your aquarium, and a good dealer will assist you in doing so.

Choosing the right system for your new aquarium can be a bit confusing, given all the different types and brands. For the marine aquarium, I absolutely recommend using several filter systems, to be sure to cover all three types of filtration.

Partial Water Changes

In nature, nitrate is used by algae as fertilizer or is converted to nitrogen gas by bacteria and removed from the water. In most aquarium systems, even with proper filtration, nitrate slowly accumulates in the water because there is not enough algae and bacteria present to use all the nitrate or convert it to nitrogen gas. Hence, nitrate must eventually be removed during frequent 5 percent to 10 percent water changes.

Inside Sponge Filter

The sponge filter is ideal for small saltwater aquariums, such as a quarantine tank. As the name implies, the filter is composed of a sponge material that is highly porous. The sponge filter sits inside the aquarium and tends to stick out like a sore thumb. Air is driven into the sponge from an external air pump and water is pulled into the filter as the air escapes.

These filters provide mechanical filtration, and they have enough surface area to support a lot of beneficial bacteria for biological filtration. The sponge itself provides the filter medium and there is no need for additional media. Sponge filters provide no chemical filtration.

Sponge filters are easy to maintain (simply rinse), are very inexpensive (less than $10), and come in sizes that can filter tanks up to 125 gallons. However, I do not recommend that you rely solely on a sponge filter. With the exception of small quarantine tanks, you need more biological filtration than one of these can provide.

External Power Filter

The external power filter is the easiest and least complicated filter system for the beginner aquarist. It looks like a big square cup, hangs on the outside of the tank, and is powered by its own motor. The cup generally contains filter floss or filter sponges and activated carbon as the filter media. Water is drawn into the filter by a U-shaped intake tube, flows thorough the filter media, and is pumped back to the tank either through a tube or a spillway.

The filter media provide mechanical and chemical filtration; biological filtration is established as the filter matures and bacteria colonize it. Therefore, the external power filter provides all three kinds of filtration. It is also specifically designed to turn over large amounts of water. The power filter also circulates the water, providing valuable aeration.

This very simple filter is easy to maintain, as most models have simple cartridges that can be routinely replaced. However, it's best to retain some of the used filter floss or use a sponge-type media so that you don't throw away all your helpful bacteria when you change the filter media.

While external power filters provide excellent filtration and are ideal for fish-only tanks, additional biological filtration is required.

External Canister Filter

This is the next step up in power filters. The canister filter is a high-powered external power filter that does not hang on the tank, but sits on the floor or under the aquarium. This filter is a self-contained high-pressure pump that draws water from the aquarium with an intake tube and sends it right back into the aquarium or into another filtration system. The filter itself contains compartments with various kinds of filter media like activated carbon, filter sponges, filter floss, and ceramic bodies. Water is pumped over all the media layers and mechanical, chemical, and biological filtration is provided. These filters are more expensive, yet provide excellent efficient filtration at a very high rate. These filters do not need to be cleaned as frequently as external power filters, and the use of multiple filter media keeps valuable bacteria when the filter is cleaned every three or four months. If you intend to house more than fish in a larger aquarium (50 gallons), the high efficiency of a canister filter is essential.

Without proper filtration, your aquarium will never be healthy.

Undergravel Filter

For decades, the undergravel filter was the standard of biological filtration. It was once considered the most efficient filter for saltwater aquariums and all successful tanks had one. However, times have changed and more advanced filtration systems are now available. Nonetheless, the undergravel filter is still considered by many aquarists to be an effective filtration choice.

The basic undergravel filter consists of a perforated plastic plate that rests on the bottom of your aquarium tank under the gravel. At each rear corner of the plate is a lift tube that extends up above the gravel. Air is pumped down each lift tube, creating a vacuum, which draws aquarium water down through the gravel and the filter plate and out the lift tube.

The gravel acts as the filter media, housing millions of bacteria that break down harmful ammonia. For this reason, certain kinds of gravel are required for this filter and a longer set-up time is necessary to establish bacterial colonies. Once a healthy filtration system is established, this filter can be used for months without intense maintenance and cleaning. The basic undergravel filter, however, has its share of problems. Debris accumulates in the gravel and needs to be routinely vacuumed to ensure that the filter does not get clogged. Cleaning can be difficult if you have a lot of corals and rocks in the tank, as well, and that's why undergravel filters are not well suited for the reef aquarium.

The undergravel filter can be improved by reversing the flow with a canister filter or by adding powerheads. A powerhead is a small pump that sits on top of the lift tube and literally pulls water through the gravel from the aquarium. This not only improves filter efficiency, but also increases water circulation.

Undergravel filters are relatively inexpensive and provide excellent biological filtration for a fish-only aquarium. If you are going to use an undergravel filter, reverse flow is the most efficient system, either with powerheads or with a canister filter.

Trickle Filter

If you plan on building a reef tank and housing invertebrates or a mix of fish and invertebrates, you will need to provide more efficient filtration. The trickle filter, also known as the wet-dry filter, was once reserved for aquarists who built their own filter systems. Now, many companies commercially manufacture a number of styles and sizes for the home aquarium.

The theory behind the trickle filter is to maximize the exposure of aquarium water to bacteria and air at the same time, so that the bacteria convert ammonia most efficiently. Basically, an overflow box on the back of the tank delivers water from the aquarium to the large acrylic trickle filter box. The filter box is generally divided into two compartments. The main compartment contains multiple layers of filter media for mechanical, biological, and chemical filtration. This compartment is mostly dry, except for the lowest few inches. The other compartment contains a pump and other optional equipment. Water from the aquarium is sprayed or trickles evenly over the first compartment through the filter media, where it collects at the bottom, or sump, moves into the other compartment, and returns to the aquarium.

Unfortunately, in most trickle filters the dry part works very well (up to twenty times better than an undergravel filter) but the wet part is not as efficient and nitrates must be removed by other means. Still, trickle filters are more efficient and effective than the filter systems I have already described. In addition, many trickle filters on the market today enable you to add other aquarium components to the second compartment of the filter, such as a heater.

Live Rock

The use of live rock as a filtration method is becoming increasingly popular. Live rock is coral rubble or reef rock that is permeated with beneficial organisms. It is either collected from wild seas around Fiji and Tonga in the Pacific or cultivated in Florida or other areas. In the United States, it is illegal to harvest wild live rock from U.S. waters, but it can be cultured. The cultured live rock is less damaging to natural reef systems, but some consider wild Pacific rock to be higher quality because it's lighter, typically more than 80 percent covered with algae, commonly sold as branches or slabs, and is more attractive (its color ranges from orange to purple).

Live rock is becoming increasingly popular as a method of filtration.

The kinds of life that can be found on live rock include bacteria, many kinds of algae, corals, sponges, snails, clams, tiny moss-like animals called bryozoans, sea squirts, crabs, barnacles, shrimps, starfish, and worms. While most of these critters are great for the tank, a couple, such as Mantis Shrimp and Bristle Worms, can be a problem.

Live rock is sold in a couple of different forms, based on its quality. Less expensive live rock is often referred to as base rock and, as the name implies, it's used as the foundation or bottom layer of the mini-reef in your aquarium. Base rock looks pretty barren, but is has lots of helpful bacteria. Decorative live rock is the expensive stuff. This is the live rock that has the most life on it—many of the critters listed above. Depending on who is marketing it, higher-quality live rock may be called fancy rock, decorator rock, algae rock, premium rock, or reef rock.

Some aquarists rely solely on live rock, an external power filter, and a protein skimmer. Bacterial colonies housed on and in the live rock provide biological filtration at very high levels. The external power filter augments the live rock and provides mechanical and chemical filtration. Live rock is easy to maintain, keeping aquariums clean for months to years with very little maintenance.

Live rock should only be added a little at a time, no more than 10 pounds at once. The total amount of live rock should not exceed 1 to 1.5 pounds per gallon, so the aquarium is not overwhelmed.

Curing Live Rock

Only place live rock in your aquarium that has been cured at some point. When live rock is harvested from the wild or from a cultivator, it's handled in many ways and many times before it gets to you. During this process, some of the life on the rock is going to die. When a piece of live rock is cured, it is held in a facility until dead and dying critters are cleared away by natural and artificial processes. Uncured live rock is harvested and shipped without this process.

If you didn't buy cured live rock from a local dealer, you are going to have to cure it yourself. The curing method involves first removing dead critters with a small brush, then isolating the rock for two to four weeks in a separate tank. Many aquarists have an isolation or quarantine tank for new fish and invertebrates, for treating animals that are sick, and for curing live rock. This doesn't need to be a complicated setup, but it should have basic filtration, a protein skimmer, and some lighting.

Water chemistry should be monitored, the water should be well circulated and aerated, and the protein skimmer cleaned frequently. Optimally, light levels should be increased slowly through the curing process, from low levels of actinic light (see page 41) in the beginning. The actinic lighting allows photosynthetic

Healthy water in your aquarium will bring out the best colors in your fish. This is an Emperor Angelfish.

organisms to thrive but doesn't provide enough light to promote the overgrowth of algae. Light should be started at six hours per day and increased by an hour every two days until you reach twelve hours. Regular water changes (20 to 50 percent every day) and frequent vacuuming are essential, as well. Monitor water chemistry daily and slowly introduce regular lighting when ammonia and nitrite levels are undetectable. When the rock is adapted to normal lighting, the curing process is complete and the live rock is ready for your main tank.

Protein Skimmer

The protein skimmer is now a standard piece of equipment in the aquarium. It uses a process called foam fractionation to remove dissolved organic wastes from the water. Basically, the protein skimmer is a tube that hangs in the back of your tank. Air is pushed to the bottom of the tube, generating a cloud of very fine bubbles that flow to the surface. Protein and other wastes adhere to the bubbles, travel to the surface, and collect in a removable cup that is emptied.

This is really a form of chemical filtration, but, unlike other filters, wastes are actually removed from the water and are not converted to something else. So the protein skimmer takes a lot of burden off the other filters.

There are a lot of protein skimmers on the market, and their effectiveness depends on how long the air bubbles are in contact with the water. Make sure your protein skimmer extends beyond the height of the tank to maximize efficiency and that it works counter to the water current.

Disinfecting the Water

There are two common methods for disinfecting water in the home aquarium: UV sterilizers and ozonators. Although some aquarists recommend one or both of them for the marine aquarium, I do not think that they are essential for the beginner.

UV sterilizers are self-contained units that kill some microorganisms that may be harmful to your fishes. Water is passed from your power filter to the UV unit, where it is exposed to ultraviolet light before being returned to the tank. However, the effectiveness of this method depends on many factors, and its usefulness for the home aquarist is not certain. UV disinfection is recommended only if you intend to maintain delicate species of fish or to treat severe outbreaks of disease.

Ozonators produce ozone, which kills microorganisms in the aquarium. However, the chemistry of ozone in sea water is poorly understood and ozone can be harmful to humans. Therefore, it is not a good idea to use ozonators to disinfect the water.

Aeration

Although most filters provide water circulation and aeration, it is a very good idea to have additional water or air pumps. Fish and invertebrates need a lot of oxygen for respiration. This is especially true for tanks with live rock filtration. Air pumps and powerheads increase circulation in the tank, promote oxygen exchange at the surface, and increase the amount of carbon dioxide, carbon monoxide, and free ammonia that is removed from the tank. In addition, high circulation maintains a uniform temperature throughout the tank.

External air pumps deliver air to the tank through air tubing and airstones. (An airstone is generally made of porous rock that allows air to pass through it, splitting the airstream into tiny bubbles.) Although they increase oxygen content and water movement, air pumps are not sufficient for reef tanks with live rock and invertebrates. These aquariums need powerheads, which are submersible pumps that dramatically increase circulation. If your tank is bigger than 50 gallons, consider two powerheads, one in each corner.

The Heater

This essential piece of equipment maintains your tank at a constant temperature regardless of the room temperature. Unless you are planning to set up a cold-water aquarium of temperate fishes, the species you will be keeping require the aquarium temperature to be maintained at 75 to 79 degrees Fahrenheit (24 to 26 degrees Celsius). Temperature, like pH, must be maintained with little fluctuation so as not to stress your tank inhabitants.

The most common aquarium heater is the submersible glass tubular heater with a built-in thermostat. This heater is attached to the side of the tank and has external controls. Once it is properly set, it automatically responds to changes in water temperature. Some models have temperature dials that are preset by the manufacturer; you then select the temperature you want to maintain. If you use one of these, I recommend that you double-check the accuracy of the dial with a thermometer.

Place your heater close to an area of high water circulation so that heated water is rapidly and evenly distributed throughout the tank. This is usually near the filter system, airstones, or powerheads.

Heater size largely depends on the size of the aquarium. The general rule is 5 watts of power for every gallon of water in an unheated room. However, most home aquariums are kept in heated rooms where temperatures do not drop suddenly and dramatically. Three watts per gallon is sufficient for heated rooms. A 30-gallon tank would therefore require a 100-watt heater. For aquariums over 50 gallons, two heaters can be used for even distribution of heat. Also, the other heater will pick up the slack if one heater fails. In this case, the calculated wattage should be divided between the heaters (70 gallons would require two 100-watt heaters).

Use a thermometer in the tank to make sure the heater is working properly.

As with all electrical components, please handle your heater with extreme care. Keep all your electrical components unplugged until the tank is completely set up and full. Do not switch your submersible heater on until it is submersed in water.

Don't rely solely on the thermostat in your heater; keep a wary eye on the temperature with an accurate thermometer. There are several kinds of thermometers for the aquarium and they are typically not very expensive. With all that circulation in the tank, try to avoid the kind that float around, bumping into things. A fixed thermometer will be where you want it to be when you want to read it.

> **TIP**
>
> Make sure you do not mix fish species that have very different temperature preferences.

Lighting

Proper lighting is a necessary component of every aquarium because it provides illumination and promotes the growth of algae. While algae are often viewed as something you need to scrape off the tank in a freshwater aquarium, the marine aquarium needs some green algae. These plant-like organisms not only consume carbon dioxide and nitrogenous wastes, they also produce oxygen and provide food to some aquarium inhabitants.

While light from the sun is the most natural, sunlight promotes too much algae growth and raises the water temperature, so aquariums should be placed away from sunlit areas of your home. Instead, buy a commercially manufactured aquarium light to illuminate the tank. Like all aquarium components, these come in a variety of types and forms.

Fluorescent lighting is by far the most common in the aquarium. Fluorescent fixtures fit snugly on top of the aquarium and provide cool light. There are several types of fluorescent tubes that can create special effects in your aquarium. Full-spectrum white tubes mimic natural daylight and are the most suitable for a fish-only marine aquarium. Marine tanks intended to harbor invertebrates should have lighting that promotes lush algae growth on live rock. The new triphospher and actinic fluorescent tubes are ideal for these aquariums.

Other types of lighting include incandescent, sodium, mercury vapor, metal halide, and tungsten lights. These provide unique types of lighting, but they all tend to heat the water and are not as economical as fluorescent lights.

An often overlooked component of the lighting system is an on/off time switch. Tropical marine fish come from regions where there is ten to fifteen hours of daylight each day. A time switch will automatically turn the aquarium

Tropical marine fish need about twelve hours of light each day. This is a Blacktail Dascyllus.

light on and off for a consistent day length. In a marine aquarium the light should be on for twelve hours.

In the wild, the sun does not rise and set like a light switch, so make every effort not to startle your fish with sudden changes in light levels. Even with an on/off timer, you can simulate a normal sunset by setting the aquarium light to go off about an hour before the other room lights do. This little detail will help keep your fish happy and, therefore, healthy.

Inside the Tank

As I have emphasized throughout this book, the majority of marine aquarium inhabitants come from tropical coral reefs. Advanced aquarists often make great efforts to duplicate specific coral reef ecosystems, such as those of Hawaii or the Caribbean, but this requires both experience and time. Since your basic marine community aquarium will likely feature a variety of fishes from several different habitats, it is best to create an aquascape that is pleasing to the human eye as well as to the fish. This requires a variety of components that will go into your aquarium and meet the habitat needs of its inhabitants.

Gravel

The bottom substrate of your aquarium will be gravel. However, unlike the gravel in a freshwater aquarium, gravel in the saltwater tank must be a specific type. Calcareous gravels have proven to be the most suitable substrate for marine aquariums. These include gravel made of coral, aragonite, and crushed oyster shells. They all contain carbonate, which helps buffer the sea water and maintain pH levels.

Grain size and gravel depth are very important and depend on your choice of filtration. If you stick with the traditional undergravel filter, your aquarium gravel should be 1 to 2 inches deep with an average grain size of about 2 to 5 millimeters (.08 to .2 inches). This substrate will be the biological filter that drives the nitrogen cycle in your aquarium. Some authors recommend using two sizes of gravel (fine on top of coarse), separated by a plastic mesh or "gravel tidy." This allows for filtration while minimizing the amount of substrate that can become clogged. The gravel tidy also protects the filter from burrowing tank inhabitants.

If you choose live rock as your primary filter, augmented with an external filter, canister filter, or sponge filter, you don't need to build a thick layer of gravel. In this case, a thin layer of ½ to 1 inch is all that is necessary. A thicker layer of gravel will trap and harbor waste, creating water-quality problems in your aquarium.

Algae

Plants play an integral role in the freshwater aquarium, but they are virtually nonexistent in the saltwater tank. This is because, with few exceptions, all of the ocean's plant life is classified in the primitive group known as algae.

Your marine aquarium needs some green algae, but you'll have to remove the overgrowth.

In your aquarium, algae can be found on the surface of the water, suspended in the water, or on the surfaces of the aquarium glass, rocks, gravel, coral, and tank decorations. Many species are introduced with live rock or coral, but some enter your aquarium with water from other aquariums and as spores.

Algae are convenient organisms because they can remove excess nutrients from your aquarium. By routinely scraping and removing some (not all) of the algae from the tank, you are physically getting nitrates, phosphates, and other excess nutrients out of your tank.

Live Rock

Earlier in this chapter I extolled the virtues of live rock. But live rock is not only an excellent filter, it also provides a natural setting for the coral reef community in your aquarium. By placing live rock in your aquarium, you are basically getting as close as you can to mimicking the natural world that your fishes come from. What better way to make them comfortable? Even if you don't use live rock as your primary means of filtration, a piece or two in your tank is a nice addition.

Coral

The next best decoration for the tropical marine aquarium, after live rock, is coral—real or artificial. Coral gives the aquarium a natural look, provides excellent shelter for tank inhabitants, and is an ideal substrate for algae growth. Real coral and other calcareous objects, such as shells, also provide the added benefit of buffering the water for pH maintenance.

Coral is basically the skeletal remains of millions of animals that once lived as a colony. On a natural coral reef, the outermost layer of the reef is the living coral colony. The reef grows as additional layers of coral are added. Coral reef growth is extremely slow, taking decades to establish. Because of this, coral reef ecosystems must be protected and living reefs should not be harvested for the aquarium trade.

> **TIP**
>
> Many aquarium stores carry corals that may have been harvested from living reefs, and it is very difficult to determine if the coral has been illegally killed. Dealers who belong to the American Marine Dealers Association (AMDA) carry products that have not been harvested illegally. These conservation-oriented dealers also make every effort not to carry fish that are endangered or captured illegally. Make sure your dealer is a member of the AMDA.

This Crested Blenny appreciates having a piece of coral to rest on.

Dead coral that has washed up on shore is perfectly suitable for your aquarium, after it has been properly cleaned. Boil all coral and other tank decorations collected from the seashore.

The alternative to dead coral is artificial coral replicas. These are becoming increasingly popular and readily available as coral reef protection efforts are increasing worldwide. These natural-looking synthetics are safe for the aquarium and provide the same benefits as real coral, with the exception of water buffering. Many large commercial aquariums use artificial coral to mimic the natural reef system. Once the artificial coral is overgrown with algae, it is virtually indistinguishable from the real thing. Most important, fish cannot tell the difference.

Most coral that you buy will be bleached white. In a natural setting and a well-balanced aquarium, this pristine look will not last. Algae colonization will add green and brown to the coral. While some beginners find this "dirty" look unappealing, be assured that it is more natural looking. However, it is a good idea to occasionally remove the algae by boiling if the growth becomes excessive and unsightly.

We have all seen beautiful photos of saltwater aquariums teeming with life, including live coral. Feeding and care of live corals require quite a bit of experience. As a novice, you shouldn't try to add live coral to your tank until you've had the chance to get your feet wet, so to speak. These invertebrate animals require exceptional water quality and can be challenging for the aquarist.

Other Decorations

Before buying any decorations for your aquarium, take the time to think about the setting you want to build for your fish. Keep in mind that the natural habitat of fish provides shelter as well as sufficient swimming space.

Other decorative materials available to the marine aquarist include tufa, a natural calcareous rock that is soft and easy to shape. It has all the beneficial attributes of coral, including buffering the water. Slate has often been used in freshwater aquariums, and it also works in the marine tank. Shells are popular natural additions to a saltwater aquarium, but be sure to boil shells before using them in your tank. Sea fans provide plant-like decorations to the aquarium, but must be soaked to expose the black skeleton before use.

Aquarium supply stores sell a variety of tank decorations that enhance your aquarium. Some are plastic or ceramic creations and others are simply well-selected rocks and stones. By purchasing these tank decorations from the dealer, you are avoiding adding items that might leech toxic substances or change the water chemistry of your tank. Avoid the temptation to collect your own rocks until you know how to identify each kind and its potential influence on the water.

More Accessories

As you develop your talents as an aquarist, you will accumulate many accessories for your tank that make your job easier and help you maintain a happy, healthy aquarium. Here are a couple of items that will give you a head start.

I have already mentioned the importance of water quality test kits. Test kits that measure pH and nitrogen compounds, such as ammonia, nitrite, and nitrate, are a must. Make sure you buy these kits when you buy aquarium components, so you will have them on hand right from the start.

There are a couple of handy accessories that help you to keep the tank clean. An algae sponge or aquarium cleaner is a sponge attached to a long handle, and is used for scraping the inside of the tank without having to empty the aquarium (or stick your arm in). The sponge will easily scrape off algae without scratching the glass. An aquarium vacuum is a must for the beginner. This is usually a hand pump siphon that extracts larger debris from the aquarium floor, so you don't have to submerse your hands or use a net.

All aquariums should be well equipped to handle fish. This means you definitely need a net or two. It's better to have a couple of sizes handy, depending on the size of your tank and the size of your fish. If your net is too small, it's difficult to corner a fish. And if it's too large, it's hard to maneuver in the tank. You will use a fish net more than you think to remove fish that are aggressive, ill, or dead.

There are other items you need for routine aquarium maintenance, and these should be within arm's length. A 5-gallon bucket and a siphon hose of adequate length are two essentials. Make sure these items are used only for your aquarium, so you don't have to prepare a clean bucket and hose every time you use one. In addition, separate cleaning tools will lessen the likelihood of introducing toxic agents into the aquarium.

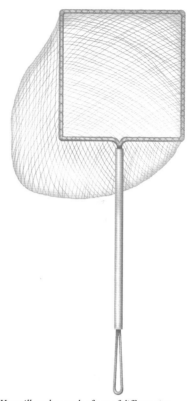

You will need a couple of nets of different sizes.

Chapter 3

Setting Up Your Aquarium

The first step in properly setting up your new aquarium is to lay out and assemble all the components in the area where you want the aquarium to be. Once you are confident that everything is in order, follow these steps to set up your aquarium.

1. Make sure everything is clean. Residue, dirt, and other toxic agents can accumulate on your equipment between the time it is manufactured and the time it gets to your home. Thoroughly rinse with clean, warm water the tank, filter (not live rock!), heater, aquarium decorations, and anything else that you expect to put in the tank. Boil aquarium decorations such as coral and shells in fresh water. Never use any kind of soap when cleaning your aquarium components; this can introduce toxins right from the start.

2. Clean the gravel. New gravel adds dust to the aquarium, making it cloudy and unhealthy. To clean gravel, empty it into a large container and fill the container with water. Thoroughly agitate the water and stir the gravel before dumping out the water. Do this several times, until the water you pour off is clear. For brand-new gravel, four to five rinses are usually enough.

3. Place the tank on its stand exactly where you want it to be. Do not expect to move the tank once it is filled with water. Now you can begin assembling the interior of your aquarium. If you are using an undergravel filter, place it in your aquarium first. Then you can begin to aquascape your tank, beginning with the lowermost layer, the gravel. Slope the gravel so that it is slightly higher in the back than in the front of the tank. This will add a natural depth of field to your aquarium.

4. Add any larger pieces of coral, rock, or other items. This is not the time for live rock. Remember, live rock houses a lot of life, so it should not go into your aquarium until the water chemistry is well balanced. Also, don't attempt to add smaller decorations until the water is added to the tank, because the filling process may disrupt them. Remember to leave spaces for heaters, filters, and other equipment.

5. This is an appropriate time to add the airstones to the aquarium, taking the opportunity to conceal air supply tubing behind larger decorations.

6. Add premixed salt water or tap water to the tank. To avoid disrupting your aquascape, place a clean plate or bowl on the substrate and pour the water onto it. In most households, tap water will be the appropriate water source. If your tap water contains chemical impurities such as nitrates, phosphates, or sulphates, or is chemically treated with chloramine, add a water conditioner, which you can buy at your aquarium dealer. If you did not premix your salt water, keep track of the amount of water used to fill the aquarium. Then add the artificial salt mix to the aquarium following the manufacturer's instructions for the amount of water you used to fill the tank.

7. Set up the filters and the protein skimmer, then position the heater in a way that maximizes its output. Place it near sources of water circulation, such as filter outlets or airstones.

8. Place the smaller decorations in the tank, add the thermometer, and fine-tune your aquascape.

9. Fit the hood, making sure the external components and electrical equipment are properly placed. Add the light on top of the canopy and make sure it is correctly hooked up.

10. When you are confident that the electrical wiring is safely insulated from sources of water, plug in the aquarium units and turn on the system. Make sure the heater is properly adjusted; this may take a day or so. Check the operation of your filters, air pumps, and light.

11. Use the hydrometer to check the specific gravity of the water. If it is a floating hydrometer, use it this way: First, transfer some aquarium water to a suitable container. This may be the plastic tube that the hydrometer came in. Make sure there is enough water to float the hydrometer.

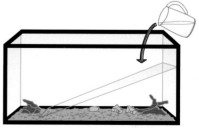

Pour water into the aquarium over a slanted surface or a plate to avoid disrupting your aquascape.

Add your live rock and let the aquarium mature before adding any fish.

Then place the hydrometer in the tube, make sure it is floating freely, and read the hydrometer at the waterline. This is the specific gravity of the water in your tank. If the specific gravity is not ideal, don't add fresh water or additional salt for twenty-four hours. This leaves time for all the salt to dissolve and to reach equilibrium. After twenty-four hours, add more salt if the specific gravity is less than 1.024, or remove some water and add tap water if the salinity is greater than 1.024.

12. Once your temperature and salinity have stabilized for a few days, add the live rock and begin to monitor your water chemistry. At this point, you still need to let the aquarium mature before adding any fish.

Aquarium Maturation

Once you have completed all these steps, your tank may be filled with water but you don't yet have the well-balanced artificial habitat that is an aquarium. You need to let the tank mature. Remember, fish need suitable water quality with ideal levels of water pH, salinity, temperature, and biological filtration. At this point, your new tank does not have a well-established nitrogen cycle, either.

You'll need to establish proper water parameters before you can add any fish. This is a Slenderspine Grouper.

These water parameters need to be established before fish can be added to the tank. Water circulation, temperature regulation, and filtration help your water to mature, but it can take as long as four to five weeks to establish bacterial colonies big enough to drive the nitrogen cycle.

After your aquarium is set up and the components are turned on, water maturation begins. When you introduce fish depends on how fast ammonia and nitrite levels peak and then drop. There are a couple of proven methods for accelerating this process so that fish can be introduced within a few weeks.

The fastest maturation of only a week or two occurs when you have well cured live rock in your aquarium. Another very effective method involves incorporating gravel from an established aquarium into your substrate. After your aquarium is set up and filled with water, go to your local aquarium store and ask for a handful of gravel from one of their systems that has been well established. Of course, make sure the store has healthy fish and well-maintained aquariums. Sprinkle their gravel on top of your gravel. This will accelerate water conditioning by "seeding" the new aquarium with bacteria.

The Nitrogen Cycle in Action

It's important to test your water daily to determine when it is properly conditioned and when you can add fish to the tank. In general, once you have seeded the tank with bacteria, the sequence of events will proceed as follows:

1. The amount of ammonia slowly increases after a few days. As ammonia builds and the bacterial colony grows, ammonia will be converted to nitrite, and those levels begin to increase. The pH level begins to fall as these other parameters rise.

2. As the bacteria population proliferates, ammonia levels decline and nitrite continues to increase. The pH should stabilize, but at a level lower than 8.2. This period can take days or weeks, depending on the amount of bacteria you used to seed the tank.

3. As ammonia is consumed by bacteria, nitrite is converted to nitrate, and that level slowly rises. Nitrite peaks and suddenly collapses as nitrate continues to rise. At this point, the tank is ready for a couple of hardy fish. But first, check the pH. The pH may remain low as the tank matures, or it may rise as nitrogenous wastes are removed. If the pH is lower than 8.0, correct it by performing a 30 to 50 percent water change. This also removes the nitrate that has accumulated in the aquarium during the conditioning process.

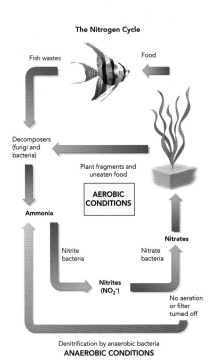

The Nitrogen Cycle

Fish wastes

Food

Decomposers (fungi and bacteria)

Plant fragments and uneaten food

AEROBIC CONDITIONS

Ammonia

Nitrates

Nitrite bacteria

Nitrate bacteria

Nitrites (NO$_2^-$)

No aeration or filter turned off

Denitrification by anaerobic bacteria
ANAEROBIC CONDITIONS

Biological filtration will not be completely established for several months, so be sure to be very conservative when you add your first fish. Start with a very small number of peaceful, inexpensive fish. Introducing very territorial fish, such as some of the Damsels, may make it difficult to add more fish, since these fish establish territories and may be aggressive toward newcomers. Closely monitor ammonia and nitrite levels after the first fish are added to make sure the biological filtration can handle the new load.

> ## Quarantine Tank
>
> Serious aquarists establish a quarantine tank for new fish so that they can evaluate the health of the fish. A quarantine tank is much smaller and simpler than the main aquarium, but it still must be properly filtered and tested routinely. The quarantine tank is also a great place to keep live rock until you are sure it is well cured and ready for your main aquarium.

Bringing Your Fish Home

When you bring a fish home, the dealer will put it in a plastic bag with water and enough oxygen for a short trip. Make sure the dealer fills the space in the bag with air. Ask to have the plastic bag placed inside a dark, opaque bag. Keeping the fish in the dark will help to reduce the stress of the trip.

Take care not to disturb or shock your fish during transport. Don't expose the bags to excessive changes in temperature or light and don't bounce them around during the trip home. You must resist the temptation to take the fish in and out of the dark outer bag to admire it. Bringing the fish from the dark into the light into the dark again will stress it. Keep it in the bag until you get home.

Placing Fish in the Tank

Follow these steps when you get home.

1. Float the plastic bag with fish in your tank so that the temperature in the bag can equalize with that of the aquarium. Let the bag sit in the tank for at least ten to fifteen minutes.
2. Open the bag and let air in. To ensure that the fish will not be shocked by the aquarium water, make sure the water in the bag and the aquarium are within 1 degree of each other. Add a handful of water from your aquarium to the bag and let it sit for another ten to fifteen minutes.
3. Add the fish to the tank by gently inverting the bag into the tank and letting the fish out.

Part II
Choosing Your Fish

Chapter 4

The Community Tank

The coral reef ecosystem is a diverse community of plants (algae), invertebrates, and vertebrate animals that function as a whole. The coral reef itself is the foundation upon which the community is built.

There are basically three general ways to stock a marine aquarium: a fish-only tank, a mixed fish and invertebrate tank (also called a semi-reef), and an invertebrate tank (known as a reef tank). With this in mind, you are faced with a wide selection of tank inhabitants, both vertebrate, like fish, or invertebrate, like shrimp.

Marine invertebrates, such as crabs, snails, coral, anemones, and shrimp, are much more sensitive to water quality than are marine fish. They also tend to be more difficult to feed and to maintain in an aquarium. When mixed with the wrong fish, some invertebrates will become a meal. When housed with too many fish, ammonia levels will kill them. For these reasons, I recommend that beginners avoid a reef tank with lots of invertebrates until they have plenty of experience. An invertebrate or two is fine, like an anemone to accompany Clownfish.

A Fish Community

You need to decide how you want to stock your aquarium—fish-only, semi-reef, or reef—early in the planning process, because your aquarium inhabitants dictate how you set up your system. Invertebrates are extremely sensitive to water quality, so any tank that houses these critters must have the highest level of filtration. Fish are a bit hardier, which makes them easier to keep. When a fish-only tank includes species that are compatible, it is called a community tank. In my opinion, beginners should start with this kind of setup because fish in the community tank are relatively hardy and get along well with each other.

A wide variety of fish are well suited to the community aquarium. The important thing is to balance the types of fishes in your tank.

T I P

Invertebrate animals lack an internal skeleton and comprise about 97 percent of all animals in the world. Insects, worms, sponges, and snails are a few examples. Vertebrates have internal skeletons and include such critters as mammals, reptiles, birds, amphibians, and, of course, fish.

Different species of fish have adapted to different lifestyles and behaviors. Some fish live anywhere in the tank, while others prefer to remain in certain areas. In

This Scarlet Cleaner Shrimp is cleaning a Butterflyfish. Think about how you want to stock your aquarium before you go shopping for your first fish.

Picking Out Healthy Fish

Tropical marine fish are more expensive than their freshwater counter-parts, and most are taken from reefs around the world and are not bred in captivity. Therefore, be selective when you get to the aquarium store. Buy fish only from healthy-looking aquariums with clear water, clean panes, and no dead or sickly fish in the tank.

Make sure the fish you want looks healthy. If the fish has any cuts, scrapes, or fin problems, don't buy it. Look for possible symptoms of dis-ease such as white granular spots, cottony white patches, frayed fins, or dull skin.

Watch the behavior of the fish. Healthy fish swim in a lively manner and are not shy. You may even want to see the fish eat before you buy it, to make sure it has recovered from the stress of shipping and has accli-mated to life in an aquarium.

It is important to introduce your fish to the aquarium in batches, buy-ing fish in lots every few weeks to a month. This allows the fish to accli-mate to one another and prevents aggressive behavior toward a single fish when it is introduced. Be sure not to stock a marine aquarium too rapidly, and follow the tank capacity guidelines outlined in chapter 3.

the community tank, you want a balance of fish throughout the tank, minimiz-ing competition and making use of the entire aquarium. In addition, many species of fish school by nature. This can be a very attractive addition to the community tank. These schooling fish should not be kept alone, but need to be in a group of at least three to six individuals.

In the next chapter I will present an overview of fish families and some indi-vidual species that make (or do not make) good community tank citizens. Keep in mind that some fish tend to be territorial or aggressive. These critters should be avoided, because a single aggressive fish in a community tank can wreak havoc on all the other species.

Some species are very compatible with other species when they are juveniles, but become solitary and aggressive as adults. These fish do not belong in the peaceful community tank.

Another aspect of choosing fish for a community tank is the maximum size of a particular species. Some species grow faster than others. You don't want to house a fish that grows 10 inches in a year. Not only does this disrupt your aquarium capacity, but the larger fish undoubtedly will dominate the tank.

Plan Ahead

When the water chemistry in your tank is well balanced and you are ready to stock your aquarium, you should have a good sense of which species you want in your tank. Don't just go to your aquarium dealer and look for fish for your tank. This can result in incompatibility among the fish. Instead, determine beforehand not only what type of critters you want, but also the species that interest you.

Take some of my suggestions in the next chapter. Consult some of the fish encyclopedias listed in the appendix. In other words, establish a list of fishes that you want to introduce into your aquarium. Remember to choose a variety of species that will live throughout the water column, from the top to the bottom.

Poor Choices for Beginners

There are many species of fish that are not well suited for the beginner's aquarium, for a number of reasons. Some are highly sensitive to the fluctuating water quality that typically characterizes the new aquarium. Others require special water conditions, such as brackish water. The beginner should not try to provide this type of specialized habitat without first acquiring some experience.

Strange and exotic creatures, like this Genie's Nudibranch, a kind of sea worm, can be very tempting. But don't start out with animals that are extremely difficult to keep.

There are also a number of species that are not socially compatible in a peaceful community tank. This group includes large carnivorous fish that eat smaller fish, territorial fish that do not tolerate trespassing tankmates, and mature fish that display aggression and combative behavior. And there are species of marine fish that exude poison when threatened. In a closed aquarium, this can have deadly consequences.

Many aggressive species are offered in aquarium stores (I have listed quite a few in chapter 5). These fish may even be promoted by dealers because smaller juveniles are considered "harmless." Don't be fooled by this argument; large predatory fish generally grow fast and develop aggressive behavior early in life.

Don't be fooled into buying fish that require special water conditions, either. These fish may live for days or weeks in your tank, but chronic stress will set in, their immune response will fail, and they will ultimately die.

As you develop your talents as an aquarist, you will be better prepared to keep some of the more sensitive species of fish. You may even want to establish an aquarium of "compatible" aggressive species or a reef tank. However, in the early stages of your aquarium-keeping hobby, it is best to concentrate on maintaining water quality with a few compatible and rugged species of fish.

Reef Tanks

Hopefully, this book is just the beginning for you. After reading it, you will have a foundation that will help you move on to more sophisticated aquarium setups.

Setting up a reef habitat can be interesting, but wait until you have some experience with saltwater aquariums. This is a Clark's Anemonefish.

Although the community aquarium can be an intriguing and exciting addition to your home, serious aquarists generally strive for more natural aquarium setups, such as a reef tank. The reef tank contains a balanced mix of fish and invertebrates. In some cases, aquarists set up a reef aquarium to closely mimic one particular habitat. It contains only fish from that habitat, invertebrates from that habitat, and substrate and decorations that mimic those found in that habitat.

Specialty tanks like this are beyond the scope of this book. However, for the serious aquarist

An Anemone Crab might live in the same habitat tank as an anemone.

who has mastered the basics with a community aquarium and would like to venture into the world of reef tanks, I recommend some of the books listed in the appendix. In these books, the authors review the many types of fish habitats that can be re-created in your home. Among them are the general community tank described in this chapter, the cool temperate water aquarium, and the tropical Hawaiian coral reef. Each habitat has its own group of resident species that live in harmony within that habitat.

Putting together a marine specialty tank does require some changes to your water chemistry, and you must be sure that your water is pristine if you are going to add invertebrates. You may need to increase your level of filtration, intensify your lighting to promote the growth of helpful algae, and bump up circulation to remove anoxic zones (areas that are deficient in oxygen). In addition, more advanced chemistry kits are required to monitor calcium, phosphate, and carbonate hardness in the water. Many species of fish eat invertebrates, so you may have to change what species are in your tank.

Setting up a reef tank can be challenging, but it is well worth the effort. However, it is always best to walk before you run. Gain some experience before running out and stocking your aquarium full of hypersensitive fish and invertebrates. They will thank you for it.

Chapter 5

The Best (and Worst) Fish for Beginners

The vast majority of marine fish sold by aquarium dealers are native to warm, tropical coral reefs. Their brilliant colors, unique body shapes, and animated behavior make these fish preferred saltwater tank inhabitants. In this chapter, we'll look at the various families of fish that commonly inhabit coral reefs and whose members may be available for your tropical fish-only marine aquarium.

This is by no means a complete list of tropical marine fish families, since there are thousands of species and hundreds of families. I strongly recommend that you consult the reference books listed in the appendix for more comprehensive information about the species listed here.

In this chapter, I will focus on tropical marine species that are relatively easy to take care of. They are well suited for the beginner's community tank, where pH ranges from 8.1 to 8.3 and temperature is maintained between 75 and 79 degrees Fahrenheit. I have listed both the common and scientific names, and have tried to include common representatives of each of these fish families. Also included is information on which level of the tank the fish is most likely to inhabit. The sizes listed below are those attained in captivity, which are generally smaller than in the wild.

Under each family I also list species to avoid in your tropical community aquarium, particularly those you are most likely to encounter in the aquarium store. With each species, I list those attributes that make them problematic for beginners.

Angelfish

Angelfish from coral reefs throughout the world are very popular aquarium fish. Some grow quite large (over 24 inches), while others don't get much longer than a few inches. Angels come in a variety of colors and patterns, which in some species change as the fish matures from juvenile to adult.

Angelfish are often confused with Butterflyfish because both have ornate colors and deep, flattened bodies. The Angels, however, belong to the family Pomacanthidae and can be readily distinguished from the Butterflies by the presence of a spine on the gill cover.

In general, Angelfish can be offered a variety of foods, but large adults can sometimes be finicky, preferring sponges and corals. The Pygmy Angels are well suited to the home aquarium, while other species of Angelfish grow larger, are prone to being aggressive and territorial as they get older, and fare better in large public displays.

Dwarf Angelfish
(*Centropyge* species)

Distribution: Atlantic, Pacific, Indian Oceans
Size: 3 inches
Food: Omnivorous
Tank level: All levels

This Golden Dwarf Angelfish (Centropyge auranticus) *is a good choice for a beginner.*

Unless you plan to keep large, boisterous fish in a high-capacity aquarium, the Dwarf Angelfishes of the genus *Centropyge* are colorful and peaceful choices for the beginner. Specifically, this group includes the African Pygmy Angelfish (*C. acanthops*), the Coral Beauty (*C. bispinosa*), the Lemonpeel Angelfish (*C. flavissima*), Herald's Angelfish (*C. heraldi*), the Flame Angelfish (*C. loricula*), and the Cherub Angelfish (*C. argi*). Unlike the larger species, many of these Angels associate in pairs and can be kept with members of the same species. These fish enjoy a variety of marine foods and they are compatible with many marine invertebrates, if you decide to diversify in the future.

Angelfish to Avoid

- Three-spot Angelfish (*Apolemichthys trimaculatus*): Delicate, territorial, difficult to acclimate and feed
- Bicolor Cherub (*Centropyge bicolor*): Delicate
- Blue-faced Angelfish (*Pomacanthus xanthometopon*): Shy, delicate
- Queen Angelfish (*Holacanthus ciliaris*): Aggressive, territorial, grows large
- King Angelfish (*Holacanthus passer*): Very aggressive, grows large
- Rock Beauty (*Holocanthus tricolor*): Very aggressive, finicky
- French Angelfish (*Pomacanthus paru*): Aggressive, grows large
- Koran Angelfish (*Pomacanthus semicirculatus*): Grows large, territorial
- Regal Angelfish (*Pygoplites diacanthus*): Delicate, difficult to acclimate

Blennies

These long, slender, very active fish belong to the family Blenniidae, which includes about three hundred species. They generally eat a variety of foods, from algae to commercial flake foods, and prefer hiding places such as caves and crevices. Most Blennies rarely exceed 4 inches long in captivity, and many are peaceful additions to a new aquarium.

Midas Blenny (*Ecsenius midas*)

Distribution: Indian Ocean, Red Sea
Size: 3 inches
Food: Omnivorous
Tank level: Lower level

Like most Blennies, this fish needs plenty of nooks and caves to hide in. Once acclimated, the Midas Blenny is quite animated, perching itself on rocks to

The Midas Blenny needs plenty of hiding places.

observe the rest of the aquarium. This yellow-hued fish swims like an eel, and its healthy appetite for all types of food makes it an ideal beginner's fish.

Bicolor Blenny (*Ecsenius bicolor*)

The Bicolor Blenny is a shy species.

Distribution: Indo-Pacific Region
Size: 3 inches
Food: Omnivorous
Tank level: Lower level

This Blenny has a front half that is dusky brown and a rear half that is orange; hence the name. The Bicolor is a shy species of fish that lives in small holes and caves. It is a pleasure to watch. When feeding, it darts from its home to catch food, quickly returning to the safety of its den by backing in. Like the Midas Blenny, the Bicolor will readily accept a variety of foods.

Blennies to Avoid

- False Cleanerfish (*Aspidontus taeniatus*): Predatory, biter
- Redlip Blenny (*Ophioblennius atlanticus*): Territorial

Butterflyfish

These popular aquarium fish belonging to the family Chaetodontidae have oval, flat bodies, terminal mouths (the mouth is on the tip of the snout), and stunning color patterns. The Butterflies are well adapted to life on the coral reef, feeding on the reef itself by seeking algae, sponges, and corals.

The Butterflyfish in general are not suitable for the inexperienced aquarist because they can be difficult to keep. Although very beautiful, these fish tend to be very sensitive to changes in water quality and they are not the hardiest of marine tropical fishes. Feeding in captivity can be difficult, and some species can be territorial. However, a couple of species are very popular in the aquarium trade and can fare quite well if water quality is properly maintained.

The stunning Threadfin Butterflyfish is also known as the Filament Butterflyfish.

Threadfin Butterflyfish (Chaetodon auriga)

Distribution: Indo-Pacific, Red Sea
Size: 4 inches
Food: Omnivorous
Tank level: Middle and lower levels

The Threadfin is named for the thread-like extension that develops on the dorsal fin of the adults. It will consume a variety of aquarium foods, and particularly enjoys live brine shrimp. Similar species include Vagabond Butterflyfish (*Chaetodon vagabundus*), Klein's Butterflyfish (*Chaetodon kleinii*), and Raccoon Butterflyfish (*Chaetodon lunula*).

Longfin Bannerfish (Heniochus acuminatus)

Distribution: Indo-Pacific, Red Sea
Size: 6 inches
Food: Omnivorous
Tank level: Middle and lower levels

This peaceful Butterflyfish is easy to keep, easy to feed, and may be kept in groups of two or three if your aquarium is large enough. The front rays of the

Young Longfin Bannerfish may help keep your other fish clean.

dorsal fin on this fish are extended and grow with age. Young of this species have been known to act as cleaner fish, removing parasites from other reef fishes at specified cleaner stations on the reef. Similar species include Schooling Bannerfish (*Heniochus diphreutes*).

Butterflyfish to Avoid

- Collare Butterflyfish (*Chaetodon collare*): Difficult to feed
- Saddleback Butterflyfish (*Chaetodon ephippium*): Difficult to feed, incompatible with others
- Banded Butterflyfish (*Chaetodon striatus*): Delicate, incompatible with others
- Copper-band Butterflyfish (*Chelmon rostratus*): Delicate, difficult to feed, needs very high water quality
- Four-eye Butterflyfish (*Chaetodon capistratus*): Delicate
- Red-headed Butterflyfish (*Chaetodon larvatus*): Delicate, difficult to feed
- Chevron Butterflyfish (*Chaetodon trifascialis*): Delicate, difficult to feed

Cardinalfish

The Apogonidae family comprises almost two hundred species of slow-moving, peaceful fish. Large eyes, two dorsal fins, and a large head are characteristic of these fish. Although nocturnal, Cardinals can be acclimated to daytime feeding and activity. When kept with other tranquil species in a community tank, these fish are well suited for the beginner.

Flamefish
(*Apogon maculatus*)

Distribution: Western Atlantic Ocean
Size: 3 inches
Food: Omnivorous
Tank level: Middle and lower levels

The Flamefish is one of the tranquil Cardinalfish that is well suited for the beginner's aquarium. This fish is a striking red color, prefers a peaceful aquarium, and takes all kinds of aquarium foods that will fit into its mouth. Since Cardinalfish are nocturnal by nature, they may be a bit shy at first. Always provide someplace for these fish to seek shelter.

The Flamefish prefers a peaceful life.

Pajama Cardinalfish
(*Sphaeramia nematoptera*)

Distribution: Indo-Pacific Region
Size: 3 inches
Food: Omnivorous
Tank level: Middle and lower levels

This species of Cardinalfish has three distinct color patterns on its body, each completely different. Like other Cardinalfish, the Pajama

The Pajama Cardinalfish has three distinct color patterns.

has large eyes for nocturnal feeding and it can be kept in groups. Care must be taken not to introduce boisterous fish with Cardinalfish, because this will disrupt their quiet lifestyle.

Clownfish and Damselfish

These fishes are very popular in the aquarium trade for hobbyists at all levels of experience. The family Pomocentridae includes the popular Clownfish and the Damselfish. The Clownfish are also called Anemonefish because they live unharmed among the stinging tentacles of anemones. The Clowns and the anemones live in harmony and both seem to receive protection from the relationship. This relationship works in the aquarium as well, but Clownfish don't need anemones to survive in the aquarium.

Damselfish are considered by many to be the hardiest of the marine aquarium species. Hence, they are often the first to be introduced into a new aquarium. These fish, however, can be territorial, aggressive, and intolerant of new tankmates when introduced too early to a new tank. Nonetheless, some of the Damsels are exciting additions to your aquarium, particularly when introduced in groups.

Ocellaris Clownfish (*Amphiprion ocellaris*)

Distribution: Indo-Pacific Region
Size: 2 inches
Food: Omnivorous
Tank level: Middle and lower levels

The Common Clownfish is the most popular Anemonefish in the aquarium trade. It feeds well on a variety of finely chopped frozen foods and can be coaxed into accepting commercial flakes. These fish are happy either alone or in pairs;

The Common Clownfish does well in pairs.

they thrive with or without an anemone. Similar species include the Percula Clownfish (*Amphiprion percula*).

Despite their name, Clark's Anemonefish can live without anemone.

Clark's Anemonefish (*Amphiprion clarkii*)

Distribution: Indo-Pacific Region
Size: 3 inches
Food: Omnivorous
Tank level: Middle and lower levels

These hardy, peaceful community fish can also live happily without an anemone. Their coloration can vary according to where they were captured. This fish will eat a variety of foods, including commercial flakes, live foods, and fresh greens. Similar species include the Tomato Clownfish (*Amphiprion frenatus*).

The Sergeant Major is a schooling species and can be kept in groups.

Sergeant Major (*Abudefduf saxatilis*)

Distribution: Indo-Pacific, Atlantic Ocean
Size: 2 inches
Food: Omnivorous
Tank level: All levels

This black-banded Damselfish is a very active schooling species that can be kept in groups. It is considered ideal for the beginner because it is hardy and accepts a wide variety of marine foods. Although the Sergeant Major is less territorial and pugnacious than other Damsels, larger individuals are aggressive toward peaceful fishes. Note that other Damsels, including the Blue Damselfish (*Chrysiptera cyanea*), the Humbud Damselfish (*Dascyllus aruanus*), the Yellowtail Damselfish (*Microspathodon chrysurus*), and Beau Gregory (*Stegastes leucostictus*), are also considered fine fish for the beginner because they are extremely hardy and easy to feed. However, these fish can be territorial as well, particularly when they grow larger, thereby creating problems for the other occupants of your tank.

Blue Green Chromis (*Chromis viridis*)

Distribution: Indo-Pacific, Red Sea
Size: 2 inches
Food: Omnivorous
Tank level: Middle levels

This is another peaceful, colorful Damselfish that can be kept in a school of three or more. The Blue Green Chromis is an active fish that may be finicky to start, but will consume a variety of chopped, meaty foods after it has acclimated to the aquarium.

Dottybacks

Fishes of the family Pseudochromidae are very similar to the Fairy Basslets in size and appearance, yet they are distributed in the Indo-Pacific while the Basslets are confined to the Caribbean. This family contains the large genus *Pseudochromis,* comprising about forty species. Unfortunately, some of the Dottybacks can be highly territorial and care must be taken to choose the right species for a peaceful marine aquarium.

The brilliant purple Strawberry Dottyback is very hardy in captivity.

Strawberry Dottyback (*Pseudochromis porphyreus*)

Distribution: Central and Western Pacific Oceans
Size: 2 inches
Food: Omnivorous
Tank level: Lower levels

The Strawberry Dottyback is a brilliant purple fish that is very easy to feed and very hardy in captivity. Like many Dottybacks, however, it can be aggressive toward similar species or similar-looking species. Therefore, it is best to have just one. It will accept most marine frozen, live, and flake foods.

Dottybacks to Avoid

- False Gramma (*Pseudochromis paccagnellae*): Very aggressive

Gobies

Somewhat similar in body shape to the Blennies, the Gobies belong to the family Gobiidae. Gobies have modified pelvic fins that are joined, forming a sucking disk. This family is the largest of the marine fishes, with more than 1,500 species and 200 genera. Some are able to live out of water for extended periods, returning to wet their gills. Like the Blennies, Gobies prefer hiding places and shelter. Some reef-dwelling Gobies act as cleaner fish. Most Gobies are brightly colored, peaceful, and relatively small. They eat a wide variety of foods.

Lemon Goby (*Gobiodon citrinus*)

Distribution: Indo-Pacific Region
Size: 1.5 inches
Food: Carnivorous
Tank level: Lower level

The Lemon Goby is a typical Goby in that it spends much of its time perched on aquarium decorations quietly observing the rest of the tank.

The Lemon Goby should not be kept with large fish.

Its coloration—beautiful yellow with blue streaks—is a nice addition to any tank. This is a very peaceful fish that should not be kept with large fish because of its small size. Once settled, the Lemon Goby accepts most foods but has a particular fondness for live brine shrimp.

The Neon Goby is known for cleaning its tankmates.

Neon Goby
(Elanctinus oceanops)

Distribution: Western Atlantic Ocean
Size: 1 inch
Food: Omnivorous
Tank level: Lower level

This Goby is well known for the cleaning services that it offers to its tankmates. This popular aquarium fish can be kept in a group of several, as long as there are no large predators in the tank. The Neon Goby is one of the few marine aquarium fish that has been bred in captivity.

Puffers

The Pufferfish look like Porcupinefish without spines, but they belong to a different family, the Tetraodontidae. They are smaller than the Porcupines and have fused, beak-like jaws. These fish also inflate to avoid being eaten, but their flesh is poisonous. Pufferfish are vigorous feeders in the aquarium, but some species can be aggressive.

Spotted Sharpnose Pufferfish (*Canthigaster solandri*)

Distribution: Indo-Pacific, Red Sea
Size: 2 inches
Food: Carnivorous
Tank level: Middle and lower levels

This Pufferfish is the smallest and most beautiful of the common puffers. It differs from the others in that it will not outgrow the tank. It is a peaceful fish that accepts a variety of finely chopped seafood. Similar species include the Sharpnose Puffer (*Canthigaster rostrata*).

Pufferfish to Avoid

- White Spotted Puffer (*Arothron meleagris*): Large, messy eater

Rabbitfish

The family Siganidae originates from the Indo-Pacific and contains two genera and about a dozen species. Their flat, oval bodies and small mouths are similar to those of Surgeonfish. In the wild, they prefer to browse on algae and other

The Foxface Rabbitfish is a vegetarian.

vegetable matter, but they can be lured into taking vegetable foods in captivity. Rabbitfish have venom glands in their dorsal and anal spines, so care must be taken when handling them. Many Rabbitfish are fast-growing and require ample swimming space.

Foxface Rabbitfish
(*Siganus vulpinus*)

Distribution: Pacific Ocean
Size: 6 inches
Food: Herbivorous
Tank level: Middle and lower levels

This is the most common Rabbitfish kept in captivity (see page 75). This fish is a vegetarian, so an aquarium with lush algal growth is preferred. It will, however, accept a variety of foods as long as vegetable matter is presented. The Foxface can be aggressive toward its own kind, so it's best to keep only one. Similar species include the Onespot Foxface Rabbitfish (*Siganus unimaculatus*) and Magnificent Rabbitfish (*Siganus magnifica*).

Surgeonfish and Tangs

These common aquarium fish belong to the family Acanthuridae. They are characterized by high profile and narrow, oval bodies. Their name is derived from the presence of two scalpel-like spines at the base of the caudal fin (tail). These are used for defense and during territorial disputes. These schooling fish are algae grazers in the wild as well as in captivity, but can be trained to take other kinds of food. In the wild, they will grow longer than 15 inches, but rarely reach half this length in captivity, depending on the species.

The Goldrim Tang has a striking black body.

Goldrim Tang
(*Acanthurus nigricans*)

Distribution: Pacific and Indian Oceans
Size: 6 inches
Food: Herbivorous
Tank level: All levels

The Goldrim's oval body and steeply sloping forehead is typical of

The Lipstick Tang is a peaceful fish.

the Tangs. This species, like other Tangs, prefers a vegetarian diet, so tank algae and vegetables are a must. This species is safe with small fish but is best kept as a single specimen in a large aquarium.

Lipstick Tang (*Naso lituratus*)

Distribution: Indo-Pacific Region
Size: 18 inches
Food: Herbivorous
Tank level: All levels

This species is another peaceful Tang that is an attractive addition to a larger aquarium. The common name refers to the red around the mouth of this fish. Remember that Tangs have two scalpels on each side of the tail, so care must be taken when handling these fish. Although the Lipstick Tang and other Tangs are herbivorous, they can be acclimated to eat protein and flake foods.

Hippo Tang (*Paracanthurus hepatus*)

Distribution: Indo-Pacific Region
Size: 6 inches
Food: Herbivorous
Tank level: All levels

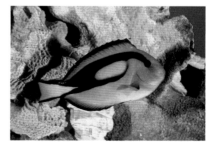

The deep royal blue and bright yellow tail of this Tang is very distinctive and has made this fish a popular

The Hippo Tang's striking good looks make it an aquarium favorite.

aquarium choice. Unfortunately, some of this coloring is lost as the fish gets older. Although some aquarists feel the Hippo can be kept with members of the same species, it is best to limit your tank to one unless you have a very large tank. These vegetarians will also accept food such as brine shrimp most of the time.

Surgeons and Tangs to Avoid

- Achilles Tang (*Acanthurus achilles*): Delicate, aggressive, not compatible with others
- Blue Tang (*Acanthurus coeruleus*): Aggressive as juveniles
- Yellow Tang (*Zebrasoma flavescens*): Highly territorial

Sweetlips

This group of fishes belongs to the same family as the Grunts, the Haemulidae. Originating in the Indo-Pacific, Sweetlips can be active like Grunts but are excellent aquarium inhabitants as juveniles, which are generally more brightly colored than adults. These fish have a quiet disposition, preferring a community tank without aggressive tankmates.

The Yellow Sweetlips is hardy but shy.

Yellow Sweetlips (*Plectorhinchus albovittatus*)
Distribution: Indo-Pacific, Red Sea
Size: 4 inches
Food: Carnivorous
Tank level: Middle and lower levels

In general, the Sweetlips are hardy but shy fishes that feed on meaty marine foods. The colors on these fish change with age. The beautiful yellow stripes fade, and the fish become browner as they get larger. This species can be reclusive if kept with boisterous tankmates, but is ideal for a peaceful tank.

Triggerfish

So named for a dorsal fin that locks into place, the Triggerfish is a member of the family Balistidae, which includes more than 130 species. These fish can be quite aggressive and they have sharp teeth that are well suited to feeding on invertebrates. They readily accept any food in captivity, but their aggressive nature renders many species of Triggerfish unsuitable for the beginner. These fish move primarily using their dorsal and anal fins, saving the tail for emergency situations.

Sargassum Triggerfish (*Xanthichthys ringens*)
Distribution: Indo-Pacific Region
Size: 10 inches
Food: Omnivorous
Tank level: All levels

This is one of the few species of Triggerfish recommended for a peaceful community tank. The Sargassum Triggerfish is a gentle fish that readily accepts all kinds of foods. It is generally safe with small fishes and is considered to be relatively easy to keep in captivity. It may, however, be difficult to obtain.

Triggerfish to Avoid

- Undulate Triggerfish (*Balistapus undulatus*): Large, very aggressive
- Queen Triggerfish (*Balistes vetula*): Belligerent, large predator
- Clown Triggerfish (*Balistoides conspicillum*): Large predator (shown on the first page of this chapter)

Wrasses

The family Labridae comprises more than 500 species that span the globe and are not confined to tropical waters. This group is quite diverse, with a variety of body shapes, behaviors, and sizes. Many Wrasse species are capable of changing sex as needed for reproductive purposes. Some are substrate burrowers that require sand, while others rest in mucus cocoons at night. Some members perform cleaning services similar to those provided by a few species of Gobies. The more active species of Wrasses can be disruptive to the peaceful tank, aggressive toward smaller fish, or too fast growing for the average aquarium.

Spanish Hogfish
(*Bodianus rufus*)

Distribution: Western Atlantic Ocean
Size: 8 inches
Food: Omnivorous
Tank level: All levels

Many of the Wrasses grow quite large, and you should take this into account when you buy one. In general, juveniles are very peaceful, hardy fish that accept a variety of marine foods. Young Spanish Hogfish are known to clean other fish. As the fish matures, its color changes to mostly red. Larger Hogfish will make a meal of smaller aquarium inhabitants, so you may need to remove them when

Spanish Hogfish can grow quite big, and adults may eat their tankmates.

they grow too large. Similar species include the Cuban Hogfish (*Bodianus pulchellus*).

Four-spot Wrasse (*Halichoeres chrysus*)

Distribution: Indian Ocean
Size: 4 inches
Food: Carnivorous
Tank level: All levels

With its bright yellow body and characteristic four black spots, this Wrasse, also called Canary Wrasse, is a beautiful addition to the beginner's aquarium. It's a hardy, peaceful fish that readily accepts a variety of frozen and live marine foods.

Wrasses to Avoid

- Longfin Fairy Wrasse (*Cirrhilabrus rubriventralis*): Aggressive
- Twin-spot Wrasse (*Coris aygula*): Grows too large, aggressive
- Harlequin Tuskfish (*Choerodon fasciatus*): Large, aggressive, predatory
- Moon Wrasse (*Thalassoma lunare*): Boisterous, large, aggressive

Families to Avoid

There are some fish families that are just not well suited to beginners, either because they are very difficult to keep, are extremely delicate, grow very large, or are downright aggressive. You may see some of these fish for sale, but they are not good choices.

Boxfish and Trunkfish

The fish of the family Ostraciidae have box-shaped bodies covered with bony plates and no pelvic fins. These fish release poisons into the water when threatened and are, therefore, a poor choice for the average aquarium. Boxfish are generally bottomfeeders and can be intolerant of their own kind. You may find the

This Spotted Boxfish secretes poison.

Spotted Boxfish (*Ostracion meleagris*) in the aquarium trade, but, like all its cousins, it is best avoided. It secretes poison and is also delicate to care for.

The Blackcap Gramma is too territorial to live in a community tank.

Fairy Basslets

There are only three species of Basslets in the family Grammatidae. These somewhat shy fish from the Caribbean prefer a lot of shelter, which they defend from other tank inhabitants. Although a beautiful addition to any tank, the Basslet's finicky habits are best suited for the invertebrate tank of the experienced hobbyist.

You may see two family members, the Blackcap Gramma (*Gramma melacara*) and the Royal Gramma (*Gramma loreto*), in the aquarium trade. Avoid them; both are highly territorial.

You may have trouble getting the Fringed Filefish (Monacanthus ciliatus) *to eat.*

Filefish

Like their close relatives the Triggerfish, members of the family Monocanthidae have a modified dorsal spine that locks into place. In contrast to the Triggers, the Filefish are more peaceful, less active, and generally smaller, making them more ideally suited to a tropical community tank. However, there may be some difficulty in getting these fish to eat in captivity, since they normally feed on coral and algae.

Particularly avoid the Long-nosed Filefish (*Oxymonocanthus longirostris*), which is delicate and difficult to feed.

Groupers and Sea Bass

Like the Grunts and Snappers, the family Serranidae is a group of fast-growing, large, predatory fishes. Most, therefore, require larger aquariums if they are to be kept for any length of time. Nonetheless, with more than 350 species in this

The Coral Hind's mouth opens wide enough to eat its tankmates.

family, there are a few smaller ones that are suitable for the peaceful aquarium of the beginner. These include the Lentern Bass (*Serranus baldwini*), the Tobacco Bass (*Serranus tabacarius*), and the Harlequin Bass (*Serranus tigrinus*). Many of the Groupers are nocturnal, spending most of their day hiding or laying low on the bottom.

Among the Sea Bass family, you may see the Coral Hind (*Cephalopholis miniata*), Speckled Grouper (*Epinephelus cyanopodus*), and Golden-stripe Grouper (*Grammistes sexlineatus*) in the aquarium trade. All grow quite large and eat their tankmates. Avoid them.

Grunts

These fast-growing, hardy fish are named for the grunting noise they make when their swim bladders amplify the sound generated by the grinding of their teeth.

Belonging to the family Haemulidae, the Grunts accept a wide variety of foods but require a lot of space. It is best to keep only small juveniles in small groups.

Lionfish and Scorpionfish

No aquarium book is complete without mentioning these unusual fish of the family Scorpaenidae, which includes more than 300 species of fish with stocky spiny heads and spiny fins armed with venom glands. They are generally predators that hover or lie in wait for prey, suddenly lunging at and engulfing it. Their camouflage coloration and body shape help them ambush their prey successfully. For obvious reasons, these fish must be handled with great care. In captivity, they are generally peaceful but will readily consume smaller tankmates. The novice is best to avoid them.

This Goldentail Moray Eel (Gymnothorax miliaris) *grows up to be big and aggressive.*

Moray Eels

These well-known, unique fish belong to the family Muraenidae. The Morays lack pectoral fins, have small gill openings, and sport long, fang-like teeth. Morays are generally nocturnal fish, feeding on other fish and invertebrates at night and spending most of their daytime hours in holes and crevices. In the wild, these fish easily grow longer than five feet, but this is not common in the average aquarium. Moray eels readily accept a variety of foods, but they are carnivorous and will consume smaller tankmates. These somewhat aggressive fish are not recommended for a peaceful community tank.

The Long-spine Porcupinefish gets too big for the average aquarium.

Porcupinefish

These oddities of the marine aquarium belong to the family Diodontidae. They have spiny scales and are able to inflate their bodies to ward off danger. Although relatively easy to keep in captivity, they generally get too large for the average aquarist.

Spiny Boxfish (*Chilomycterus schoepfii*), Long-spine Porcupinefish (*Diodon holacanthus*), and Common Porcupinefish (*Diodon hystrix*) do turn up in the aquarium trade. All are large and predatory, and the Common Porcupinefish is also a messy eater.

Seahorses and Pipefish

These exotic fish of the family Syngnathidae are no strangers to the aquarium trade. The Pipefish lack the characteristic prehensile tail, vertical swimming position, and angled head of the Seahorse. The group is characterized by unusual reproductive behavior, in which the female deposits eggs into an

Seahorses are beautiful to watch, but are too delicate for the beginner aquarist to keep.

abdominal pouch on the male. They are then fertilized and incubated by the male in his pouch.

Unfortunately, Seahorses and Pipefish have feeding and water-quality requirements that make it difficult for the beginner to keep them for any length of time. They do not compete well with other species for food. These fish are very peaceful and do best in a very quiet aquarium.

You will see Banded Pipefish (*Doryrhamphus dactyliophorus*), Florida Seahorses (*Hippocampus erectus*), and Common Seahorses (*Hippocampus kuda*) for sale. Although they are exotic and beautiful, all are delicate and difficult to keep.

Sharks

There are at least 31 families and 375 species of Sharks in the world, most of which have never been kept in aquariums. Sharks, in general, get too big for the home aquarium, can be very aggressive, and are very sensitive to water quality. For these reasons alone, sharks are not recommended for beginners.

The Emperor Snapper will quickly dominate an aquarium.

Snappers

The family Lutjanidae, which includes more than 200 species, is another group of fast-growing, highly active fish that are not suitable as adults for the average marine aquarium. Several species of this family are commercially exploited for food throughout the world. These fish are predatory by nature, require a lot of space, and will quickly dominate an aquarium. The Emperor Snapper (*Lutjanus sebae*), a large, predatory fish, does turn up in aquarium stores.

Squirrelfish

These vibrant red fish of the family Holocentridae are nocturnal in the wild, using their large eyes to help them feed at night. In the aquarium, they can be conditioned to eat during the day. Their long bodies have two dorsal fins: a longer fin of spines and a shorter, soft-rayed fin close to the tail.

Squirrelfish need a lot of space to accommodate their highly active nature. They can be disruptive to a peaceful community tank and, as they get larger, they may consume smaller fish. You may see the Common Squirrelfish (*Holocentrus adscensionis*) for sale, but it poses the same problems as all the members of its family.

This Longjaw Squirrelfish (Sargocentron spinifer-unu) *is very active and needs a lot of space.*

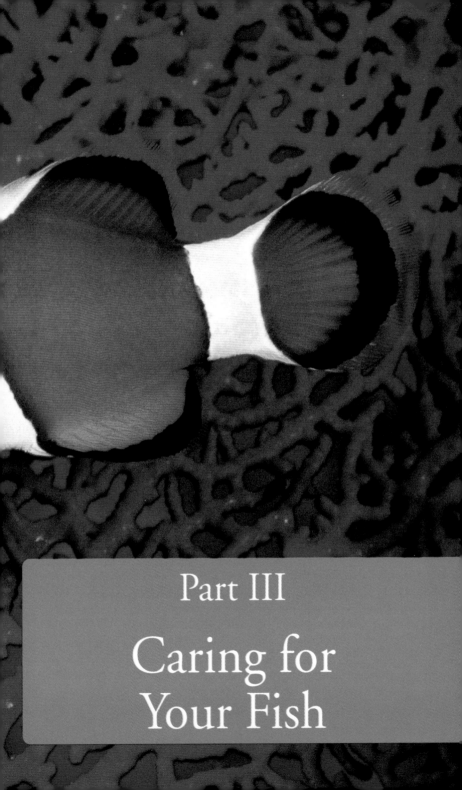

Part III

Caring for Your Fish

Chapter 6

Feeding Your Fish

The raw materials needed for life and growth are called nutrients. Fish, like all animals (and plants), need these nutrients for sustenance, growth, and reproduction. They can only get these nutrients by eating plants or other animals.

There are many things to take into account when it comes to providing food for your fish. In their natural habitat, fish have evolved various feeding strategies to optimize their ability to obtain nutrients. With all the different kinds of fish and habitats, you can just imagine how many kinds of feeding strategies there are. But in general, fish can be divided into three groups based on the type of feeding strategy they use.

Dietary Needs of Fish

Like all living animals, fish have dietary requirements for the basic building blocks of life: protein, fat, carbohydrates, vitamins, and minerals. In their natural environment, fish forage to meet their dietary needs. In the home aquarium, they rely entirely on you to bring home the bacon. Unfortunately, the exact nutritional requirements of tropical marine fish are very poorly understood. These requirements can differ by species, age, water temperature, and many other factors. The best that any aquarist, including the professionals, can do is to feed the fish a variety of foods to approximate these requirements.

There are many different types of foods available for your tropical marine fish. Carnivores will eat flake food, brine shrimp, and almost any kind of

Feeding Strategies

You can divide fish into three groups based on the kind of feeding strategy they use: carnivores, herbivores, and omnivores. Carnivores only eat other fish and invertebrates. In an aquarium, many carnivorous fish will eat dead food, commercially prepared pellets and flakes, and live critters. Pieces of fish, shrimp, and other meats may appeal to some carnivores. But some species will simply not accept anything but live food. Guppies, Goldfish, and Brine Shrimp are commonly offered to these predators. (The Lionfish on the first page of this chapter is one of these carnivores who eat their tankmates.)

Herbivores eat only vegetable matter, which includes flake foods and other types of plant matter, including algae. Omnivores eat a variety of foods and have no specific dietary preferences. They will eat flakes, live foods, and bits of table food. Basically, they will eat almost anything. They are clearly the easiest group to feed and are thus the most highly recommended for the beginning aquarist. You probably noticed that many of the species I recommended in chapter 5 are omnivorous.

seafood—crab, lobster, oysters, and clams. Herbivores will adapt to an omnivorous life, taking flake and frozen foods and vegetables, while grazing on aquarium algae. The omnivore will eat all these foods.

Aquarium foods can be grouped into several categories. For marine tropicals, I prefer to lump aquarium foods into three general categories: natural foods, prepared foods, and live foods.

Natural Foods

As the name implies, natural foods include items that are obtained fresh, frozen, or freeze-dried with little to no processing. These are typically leafy green vegetables, fish and invertebrate flesh, and thawed or freeze-dried brine shrimp and other plankton.

This Midas Blenny has a healthy appetite and will eat just about anything.

Leafy Green Vegetables

It is essential to provide vegetable matter for herbivorous fishes. Algae in your aquarium are great for grazing fish. You can also feed a variety of vegetables fresh, blanched, or thawed, including lettuce, spinach, cabbage, parsley, kale, and watercress. Some experts recommend blanching the vegetables to aid digestion. In general, vegetables are composed mostly of water and are low in energy, proteins, and fats, but contain high concentrations of carbohydrates, fiber, and certain vitamins. You should not feed your fish exclusively vegetables. It's always a good idea to rinse any vegetables thoroughly before feeding them to your fish, to wash off any pesticide residue.

Fish and Invertebrate Flesh

This category includes a variety of seafood that is fed fresh, thawed, or cooked. Cooking these foods does not lower their nutritional value, and it is a good idea to do so because raw seafood can carry infectious diseases to your fish. Boiled, steamed, or canned (not in oil) seafood is fine. You should generally stick to seafood (from the ocean) when feeding marine fish, because their tissue is of a similar composition.

The variety of meats available is vast and can include fish such as herring, anchovy, smelt, mackerel, and tuna, and shellfish such as clams, shrimp, mussels, scallops, oysters, crabs, and squid. Meaty foods tend to contain less water and carbohydrates and substantially more protein and fats than vegetable matter. This is a must for carnivorous fish.

Frozen and Freeze-dried Foods

These foods often constitute the greatest portion of your fish's diet because they are specifically processed for aquarium use and are widely available. Some of the most common commercially available frozen foods in this category include brine shrimp, krill, and other shrimps. Most commercial processors treat these animals with gamma rays to ensure that they are disease free. They keep for several months in the freezer and can be thawed as needed. The dietary value of this food is similar to that of meaty food.

Freeze-drying has made it possible to preserve a variety of natural foods for aquarium fish. For the marine aquarium, the process has most often been applied to brine shrimp and other small invertebrates, such as krill. While these items increase the variety of food for your fish, they should not be the only food offered. Although freeze-dried brine shrimp have the same fat concentrations as freshly killed brine shrimp, it has not been proven that they are a complete dietary substitute for live brine shrimp.

This Bangaii Cardinalfish is an omnivore, and will eat a wide variety of foods.

Prepared Foods

As you would guess, this category of food includes processed flakes and dried food for aquarium fish. Commercially prepared foods make every effort to approximate the three basic dietary requirements: proteins, fats, and carbohydrates. They are also supplemented with vitamins and minerals. These foods come in many varieties, depending on the type of fish (carnivore, herbivore, omnivore) you are feeding, and new formulations are added every year to better meet the dietary needs of your fish.

Prepared foods also come in many forms, depending on the size and feeding behavior of the fish. Flakes, tablets, pellets, and crumbs are available. Larger predatory fishes should be fed pellets as opposed to flakes because they prefer to consume a large quantity. In addition, fish that feed on the bottom may not venture to the surface for flakes, so they must be fed pellets or tablets that sink to the bottom. Pellets can also be stuck to the aquarium glass for the grazing species in your tank.

Many of the community fish reviewed in this book can be fed prepared foods. However, if you want active, colorful, healthy fish, you must vary their diets. Flakes are best as a staple food, but you should also add other natural and live foods daily to enrich your fish.

Live Foods

Live food is an excellent source of nutrition for the tropical marine aquarium. Fish fed live foods usually grow faster and have higher survival rates. This is because live foods retain active enzymes that make digestion more efficient. Many aquarists believe live foods are an essential requirement of captive fish and should be fed at least as a dietary supplement. The kind of live food you offer will depend on the size of the fish you are feeding. Small fish, such as freshwater Guppies and Goldfish, are often fed to large predatory fish such as Lionfish.

Brine Shrimp

By far the most popular live food for the tropical marine fish is brine shrimp. The brine shrimp (*Artemia* species) is a primitive crustacean that inhabits salt pans in more than 160 locations around the world. Those in your local aquarium store probably originated in San Francisco Bay or Great Salt Bay in Utah. They are one of the best sources of nutrition available for fish of any type, because they provide fats and protein. Of all the live food available, they are the safest because they do not carry disease.

This Blue Devil Damselfish likes to eat a wide variety of foods.

An added advantage to brine shrimp is that you can raise them yourself. You can buy brine shrimp eggs at a good aquarium supply store. To raise brine shrimp, it is best to follow the instructions accompanying the eggs.

How to Feed Your Fish

The biggest feeding problem for the beginner aquarist is knowing how much and how often to feed. Some fish are gluttons while others will stop when they are sated. Follow the guidelines below when feeding your fish and you will develop a working sense of how much and how often to feed.

1. Offer as much food as your fish will eat in five minutes. Flakes should sink no deeper than one-third the height of the tank. Provide tablets or pellets for bottom fish.
2. Feed your fish in very small portions over the five-minute period.
3. If you are home during the day, feed your fish small portions over the course of the day. If you are not home, feed your fish twice a day at the same times every day—once in the morning, once at night.
4. Always feed your fish at the same spot in the tank.

5. Do not overfeed your fish, no matter how much you think they need
   more food. Overeating will stress your fish and cause detritus to accumulate in the tank, degrading water quality.

Watch all your fish during feeding and make sure that each gets its share of
food. Remember that fish have different mouth shapes that enable them to feed
at different levels in the tank. Some
species will not go to the surface to
eat, and wait for food to disperse
throughout the tank. Don't rely on
surface feedings and the leftovers of
others to feed bottom fish. Use pellets or other foods that sink to the
bottom for these fish.

> **TIP**
>
> Too much food is bad for your fish
> and bad for your aquarium. It is def-
> initely better to feed too little than
> too much.

Remember, refusal to eat is one of the first signs of illness, so keep an eye out
for fish that seem to have no interest in food.

Try using flake food and frozen brine shrimp as your staples and mix in a
variety of foods as your fish acclimate to your aquarium. Try not to feed your
fish right after turning on the light; they won't be fully alert until about thirty
minutes later. In addition, make sure you match the size of the food with the

*The ocean is an eat-or-be-eaten world. Some fish eat small shrimp. This Banded Coral Shrimp eats
small shrimp as well.*

size of the fish's mouths. You may need to crush the food for fish with small mouths. Be sure not to grind the food too small, because this adds fine particles to the water that degrade water quality. Always remove food from the tank that has not been consumed.

If you are going to be away from your aquarium for one or two days, the fish will be fine without food. For longer periods, make arrangements for someone to feed your fish. Prepare portions ahead of time and give detailed instructions on how to offer food properly. Do not let them feed your fish at their own discretion unless they are experienced aquarists. Remember that it is better to underfeed than to overfeed your fish.

Chapter 7

Maintaining Your Aquarium

You planned your aquarium, bought your equipment, set up your tank, established excellent water quality, carefully selected and introduced the fish, and fed them well. Now it's time to keep your fish healthy by maintaining the quality of their new home.

Aquarium maintenance involves everything from turning the light on and off and feeding the fish every day to spending time observing your fish. Watching is the fun part, of course—that's why you have an aquarium, after all. But it's also important to get to know your fish, watch how they interact, make note of any unusual behavior, check the fish closely for any signs of disease and look for clues that one or more may be aggressive.

The more stable the conditions in your aquarium, the less likely you are to cause stress among its inhabitants. Rapid fluctuations in water temperature and water quality cause stress and compromise the health of your fish. Make it a point to monitor the water temperature and make sure it remains constant. Check the water level and specific gravity, as well. Remember that water should be topped off as often as necessary with tap water.

Examine the filter, heater, and airstones to make sure they are in working order. The thermostat light in the heater should be working properly. The air pump and airstones should be operating at maximum efficiency. Empty the protein skimmer cup if organic waste has accumulated.

These things should be checked daily and require just a few moments of your time. While you are feeding or simply enjoying your pets, you can perform a routine check of the tank components and the aquarium occupants.

Vacuum

Vacuuming is one of the most important parts of maintaining your tank. You must reduce the accumulation of detritus (also called mulm) in the gravel so that your filtration systems remain effective. Mulm is the combination of fish wastes and uneaten food that decay on the bottom of the aquarium. If it is not removed, this organic waste ultimately breaks down into ammonia and nitrites and overwhelms the nitrogen cycle. This will disturb your water chemistry, potentially harming your fish. If detritus is allowed to accumulate to excessive levels, your filters clog and water quality declines quickly. If you use an under-gravel filter, too much mulm clogs it and prevents water from flowing through the gravel, reducing the filter's efficiency.

Aquarium vacuums, sometimes called substrate cleaners, are available commercially. I recommend using a wide hose to siphon wastes while you are doing a water change (see page 100). This accomplishes two goals at once: vacuuming mulm and removing water from the tank for a partial water change. When you vacuum, make sure you rake the gravel gently and don't mix it up too aggressively.

Bottom-dwellers like this Midas Blenny will appreciate regular vacuuming to keep the substrate clean.

> ## It's a Commitment
>
> Cleaning an aquarium involves an active, conscientious effort on your part. In fact, maintaining a fish tank is not for the lazy. Don't set up a tank if you don't intend to follow through and keep it clean and healthy. All too often, interest wanes after the first couple of months and the aquarium occupants ultimately suffer the consequences. Realize that going into this hobby requires a real commitment on your part. Concern must be shown at every step and on every level. Your fishes' lives depend on your attention.

Check the Filter

If you have an external filter, it is very important to check the filter media. The top-level mat gets dirty easily and quickly, since this is the level that collects the largest pieces of debris. An excessive build-up of detritus in your filter inhibits flow and ultimately reduces the filter's effectiveness.

Rinse the filter mat every three or four months under lukewarm water until the water runs clear. You should probably replace about 50 percent of the filter media every six months, making sure to reuse about half the old filter material. You have an established bacterial colony in your filter media and you don't want to throw it all out and start from scratch. One of the most common mistakes hobbyists make is to replace the entire filter contents every couple of months because it looks dirty. Some of that "dirt" is bacteria that are beneficial to the filtering process.

For filters that use cartridges as media, check with the manufacturer for optimum maintenance and how often they should be replaced. The activated carbon in the filter should be good for about two months, and then it should also be replaced.

Algae

Throughout this book, I refer to algae as a friend of the marine aquarium—if it does not get out of control. Algae removes nitrate from the water and provides food for some of the naturally herbivorous fishes. But what exactly are algae and are all algae beneficial?

Algae make a tasty snack for this Copper-Banded Butterflyfish. You just need to make sure the algae growth does not get out of control.

Algae are photosynthetic organisms that occur throughout the world in many habitats, ranging from freshwater to marine and from the Arctic to the Equator. For many years, algae were grouped with the fungi into the class of plants known as *Thallophyta*. More recently, scientists have classified these plant-like organisms into their own kingdom, called the *Protoctista*.

Algae are relatively simple organisms that range in size from the one-celled microscopic types to large seaweeds that grow to more than 230 feet long. They are also very hardy organisms and have a tremendous reproductive capacity. They can enter your aquarium as spores, borne by the air or carried by tank furnishings from another aquarium.

Algae have adapted to all kinds of water conditions. They are important as primary producers at the base of the food chain. They provide oxygen and food for aquatic life, but some forms can contribute to the mass mortality of other organisms. In tropical regions, coralline algae can be as important as corals in the formation of reefs.

One thing is for sure: not all algae are alike. There are a number of formal classifications for algae, and scientists have recognized at least eight major divisions, but not all occur in the average aquarium. Some kinds are desirable and others are not. Some are typically referred to as seaweeds, others are planktonic, and some are both. Let's take a closer look at the types you are most likely to encounter or purchase for your marine aquarium.

Green Algae

This group is called the *Chlorophyta*. With 7,000 species, this is the most diverse group, but only about 10 percent of the green algae species are marine forms. These are typically the most beneficial algae, although some species are less desirable because they can cloud water or grow out of control. They are green because they contain chlorophyll, just as higher forms of plants do.

The planktonic spores of green algae are not visible to the naked eye and appear as a green cloudiness in the water. These spores will sometimes form a green film on the aquarium glass. Larger green algae come in desirable plant-like shapes or less desirable hair and mat-like forms. The most desirable species of green algae are cultivated and sold as attractive additions for your aquarium. Some of the desirable forms of algae include species of *Caulerpa, Halimeda,* and *Valonia.*

Red Algae

This group of algae, called the *Rhodophyta*, contains about 6,000 species. Most are marine seaweeds. Although most red algae are multicellular and grow attached to rocks and other algae, there are some single-celled forms. Red algae are red because of the pigment phycoerythin, which absorbs blue light and reflects red light. Their coloration depends on how much of this pigment they have, and may range from reddish yellow to bright red to greenish blue and

If your water becomes cloudy, you won't be able to enjoy the spectacular colors of your fish, like this Candystripe Dwarf Angelfish.

brown. Since blue light penetrates much deeper in the water than red light, these algae typically live at deeper depths and are well adapted to low lighting conditions.

Most red algae are introduced into the aquarium on live rock. The most common are called coralline red algae, which secrete a hard calcareous shell just as corals do. These algae are considered very important in the formation of tropical reefs and in some areas may contribute more to reef structure than do the corals themselves. They are beneficial to the aquarium, encrusting rocks and even spreading to the fixtures and glass.

Brown Algae

Belonging to the group *Phaeophyta*, the brown algae comprise about 3,000 species that are predominantly marine seaweeds. There are no single-celled forms of brown algae, and the simplest is a branched filamentous organism.

Their brown coloration results from the dominance of the pigment xanthophyll, which masks other pigments such as chlorophyll. Colors range from pale beige to yellow-brown to almost black. Some forms of brown algae come attached to live rock when you buy it. Like the red algae, brown algae are generally beneficial for the saltwater aquarium.

Diatoms

These algae of the group *Bacillariophyta* are microscopic cells composed of overlapping half-shells of silica. These are the diatoms, planktonic (free-floating) and benthic (bottom-living) algae that float in the ocean or are in the sediment. Their silica shells, called frustules, are geometric in shape, but their microscopic size makes it difficult for the average aquarist to see them.

These algae proliferate in aquariums with high nitrate levels. They are usually the first algae to establish themselves. Diatoms form a brown slime on the gravel, rocks, decorations, and aquarium glass. Heavy concentrations of diatoms will discolor the water. As the aquarium matures, these algae should disappear. Until they do, you should scrape them away to keep a clear view of your aquarium pets.

Dinoflagellates

Members of the group *Dynophyta* are single-celled organisms that have the characteristics of both plants and animals. The name dinoflagellate refers to the forward swimming motion created by their tails, which are called flagella. Not all species of dinoflagellates are photosynthetic; some are planktonic, while others live on the bottom. A few species of dinoflagellates are harmful to sea life and those that consume it. Dinoflagellate blooms, called red tide, turn coastal waters reddish-brown, producing serious toxins that can harm human health.

In some instances, excess nutrient levels cause dinoflagellate blooms in an aquarium. This will result in brown mucus-like slime covering most of the tank and its contents. If this happens, the algae must be physically removed with a siphon and you should conduct a 50 percent water change.

The dinoflagellates called zooxanthellae live in live corals, sponges, clams, and anemones. These algae form a symbiotic relationship with their hosts, providing a food source of organic carbon that they produce during photosynthesis.

Blue-green Algae

The blue-green algae are not algae at all, they are bacteria. For years, they were considered algae because they are aquatic and they make their own food. This group of bacteria is called the *Cyanobacteria* and it has the distinction of being the oldest known group of fossils—more than 3.5 billion years old. Because they are bacteria, blue-green algae are small and single-celled, but they grow in colonies that are large enough to see. Although called blue-green algae, their colors can range from black to red to purple.

Blue-green algae can be beneficial in your substrate, if your aquarium is otherwise healthy. This is an Orange-Spotted Blenny.

Like a lot of bacteria, blue-green algae in your substrate are beneficial to the health of your aquarium, feasting on detritus. However, in tanks with poor water quality, high nutrients, and poor circulation, they form a dark brownish-red gelatinous mat called red slime on rocks, gravel, and plants in your tank. They are also capable of producing toxins that poison aquarium fish. If allowed to proliferate, they will smother the tank. Unfortunately, few critters feed on blue-green algae, so they must be physically removed with a siphon during a partial water change.

Test the Water

When you first set up the aquarium, testing the water every couple of days is critical to monitoring the maturation process. When you begin to add fish, water chemistry changes radically and monitoring water quality is critical to the survival of your fish.

After this sensitive period of two to four months, it is still very important to test your water, and I recommend that you do so every two weeks. Testing gives you a good understanding of the nitrogen cycle and lets you know when a water change is needed. Sudden behavioral changes in your fish, disease, mortality, excessive algae growth, and smelly or cloudy water all warrant an immediate water quality test and a possible water change.

Partial Water Changes

Partial water changes are one of the most important aspects of cleaning and maintaining your tank. When you do a water change, you remove some of the aquarium water and replace it with properly balanced artificial sea water. The amount you change will vary with the quality of your tank and with the frequency of water changes. Some experts believe a 5 percent water change is sufficient every two weeks, while others believe this volume should be up to 20 percent. I recommend that you start with a water change of 10 percent every two weeks, and adjust this amount depending on water quality.

Water changes help maintain excellent water quality because you dilute the amount of nitrogenous compounds (nitrites and nitrates), harmful gases, and other toxic substances each time you conduct one. The water you add, which should be the proper specific gravity, replaces exhausted trace elements and nutrients, as well.

The best way to change aquarium water is to use a siphon and a large bucket. The siphon is basically just a 3- or 4-foot hose or tube that will transfer water from the tank to the bucket.

How to Siphon

1. Fill the tube completely with water, making sure there is no trapped air in the tube. Make sure the siphon is clean and that your hands are clean, too. You can fill the hose by submerging it in the aquarium, but only do this if your aquarium is large enough to accommodate the hose without spooking the fish. Otherwise, place one end of the tube in the tank and apply suction to the other end to start the flow.
2. Make sure the bucket end is lower than the aquarium, or the siphon will not work. If you filled your siphon in the aquarium, plug one end of the hose tightly with your thumb, lift it from the aquarium, and bring it lower than the tank to the bucket.
3. Release your thumb and the water will begin to flow rapidly from the aquarium into the bucket.

As I mentioned earlier, use the siphon to remove debris from the tank while you are making a water change. The surface gravel should be stirred just before every partial water change, for two reasons. First, it breaks up impacted areas

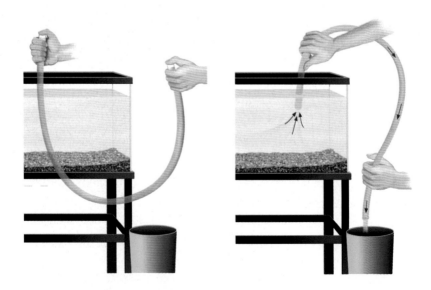

Maintenance Checklist

Daily

- [ ] Feed the fish twice a day; remove any uneaten food.
- [ ] Turn the tank lights on and off.
- [ ] Check the water temperature.
- [ ] Check the heater and make sure the thermostat light is working.
- [ ] Make sure the filter(s) is working properly.
- [ ] Make sure the aerator and powerheads are working properly.

Every Other Day

- [ ] Check the protein skimmer and empty the cup, if necessary.
- [ ] Top up the water level with tap water.
- [ ] Remove excess algae from the glass.

Weekly

- [ ] Study the fish closely, watching for behavioral changes and signs of disease.
- [ ] Check the filter to see if the top mat needs to be replaced.
- [ ] Clean the cover glass.
- [ ] Measure specific gravity with the hydrometer.

Every Other Week

- [ ] Change 10 percent of the tank water.
- [ ] Vacuum the tank thoroughly and remove mulm and detritus.
- [ ] Test the water for ammonia, pH, nitrite, and nitrate.

Monthly

- [ ] Rake through the coral sand.
- [ ] Rinse any tank decorations that have excess algae.
- [ ] Remove excess algae.

Every Other Month

- [ ] Change the filter carbon and some floss.
- [ ] Clean the protein skimmer.

Quarterly (Every Three Months)

- [ ] Replace the airstones.
- [ ] Rinse the filter media completely and replace some of them, if necessary.

where anoxic zones (areas with little oxygen) have developed. Second, it puts detritus into suspension where it can be siphoned out with the old water.

When it is time to add water, it is best to use aged water that has been pre-mixed and stored in a cool, dark place. Make sure the water you add is the same temperature and specific gravity as that of your aquarium.

Replace the Gravel

If you have a freshwater aquarium, you are encouraged to break it down completely every year, essentially starting from scratch. This is not the case with a marine aquarium. A well-established biological filter will be effective for years. However, if you use an undergravel filter it may become heavily clogged after a long period of time. The substrate itself may begin to break down as well.

If this happens, you can slowly replace the gravel over several months by removing a thin strip of gravel and replacing it with new gravel. The next week, repeat the procedure, and so on until the entire substrate has been replaced without disrupting the aquarium. Under no circumstances should you break down a healthy aquarium and replace all the gravel at one time.

Chapter 8

Tropical Marine Fish Diseases

If you plan to be a tropical fish hobbyist for some time, it is inevitable that one of your fish will become infected with some kind of disease. Marine tropical fish are subject to all kind of maladies. Pathogenic organisms, including parasites, bacteria, viruses, and fungi, are present in all aquariums. Many are introduced with new fish and some are highly contagious. However, disease only breaks out if the resistance of your fish is diminished. Poor living conditions weaken your fish, cause chronic stress, and ultimately lower the fish's resistance. That is when your fish are most vulnerable to disease.

This is why I emphasize the importance of maintaining a healthy aquarium for your pets. Stress caused by capture, handling, fasting, crowding, and injury renders your fish vulnerable to disease. Even though you may have done everything possible to keep a disease-free environment in your tank, your fish may still get sick. Even the experts experience some problems.

The first step to treating any kind of ailment in your aquarium is to recognize and identify the problem. You can identify a fish that is not healthy by its appearance and behavior. Since you're spending time watching your fish while you feed them, you should be able to identify problems as soon as they manifest themselves. External symptoms include a number of physical abnormalities of the head, body, fins, gills, scales, and anus. Telltale behavioral signs of illness include:

- Loss of appetite
- Hyperventilation of the gills
- Gasping for air near the surface
- Erratic swimming behavior

- Lack of movement
- Rubbing the body or fins
- Twitching the fins

Commercial Remedies

It is very important to use commercially available treatments instead of home-made remedies. Some experts recommend chemicals such as malachite green or potassium permanganate for treating diseases. These chemicals must be handled in very exact dosages. Overdosing a fish with one of them will kill the fish more rapidly than the disease. That's why commercial remedies are a much better choice.

Discuss all the possible remedies for a disease with your local aquarium dealer and let that person advise you on the best commercial remedies avail-able. If you are still not satisfied, don't be afraid to call your veterinar-ian and ask a few questions. If your veterinarian does not treat fish, he or she can usually recommend someone who does.

> **TIP**
>
> When you apply any commercial remedy, make sure you follow the directions exactly.

Treatment Methods

If disease does strike one of your fish, there are a few methods for treating it. These include direct aquarium treatment with therapeutic agents, the hospital tank, the dip method, and internal medication. Unfortunately, the best remedy for disease in the marine aquarium is prevention. Sometimes, despite all your efforts and the application of commercial remedies, the fish will die.

Direct Aquarium Treatment

This involves applying therapeutic agents directly into the aquarium with the diseased fish. Sometimes called the long bath, this method can be effective against some diseases, but not always. In some cases, medications may be absorbed by the aquarium decorations or filter media, or they may be toxic to filter bacteria and invertebrates. In these situations, it is best to isolate the infected fish in a hospital tank.

The Hospital Tank

In chapter 3, I mentioned that some aquarists isolate new fish in a quarantine tank. This way, the fish can be evaluated for signs of disease before introducing them into the main aquarium. I recommend that you set up such a tank to isolate individuals suffering from disease. This tank will reduce the likelihood of the disease spreading to other

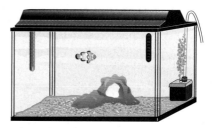

A hospital tank should be small and sparsely decorated, but make sure to include some hiding places for the fish.

animals in the aquarium. It will provide refuge for a fish that may be harassed by healthier fish. The hospital tank will also make it easier to treat the fish without subjecting other fish and invertebrates to the treatment, and it will make it easier to observe and diagnose the ailing fish.

The hospital tank need not be large; a 10-gallon tank will do. It does need adequate filtration and aeration, but elaborate decorations and gravel should be left out. For the fish's security, try to provide some kind of cover in the form of rocks or empty flowerpots. An internal sponge filter or external power filter will be sufficient for the hospital tank.

The Dip Method

This method can be very stressful to the fish. It involves removing the infected fish from the aquarium and dipping it into a bath containing a therapeutic agent or just fresh water. The dip is brief enough not to injure the fish but long enough to kill the pathogen. Unfortunately, this method does not treat the infected agents in the aquarium, just the fish.

The bath is prepared by filling a 1.5-gallon container full of fresh water that has been conditioned to match the temperature and pH of the main aquarium. The pH can be elevated by adding sodium bicarbonate to the container. Add a quart of sea water to the bath, as well, to reduce the osmotic shock to the fish. Net the fish and place it in the container for three to ten minutes. It may show signs of disorientation for a moment, but it should recover. Immediately transfer the fish back into the aquarium if it cannot maintain its balance.

Internal Medication

Some remedies need to be administered internally. This is usually accomplished by injecting the fish or feeding it the remedy. Giving your fish an injection is not recommended for the average home aquarist.

Sometimes, despite your best efforts, a sick fish will still die. That's a very good reason to keep your tank and its inhabitants healthy in the first place. This is a Square Anthias.

Feeding the fish food that has been medicated can be very difficult as well. In many cases, the dosage is difficult to estimate, the fish is not eating normally, and you cannot guarantee that the fish being treated is getting the proper amount of food. This treatment method is, therefore, only marginally successful and should be avoided by the beginner.

Common Treatments

The number of treatments available to the home aquarist is somewhat limited for marine fish diseases. The fact of the matter is that many are successful only some of the time.

Copper

Copper is a pollutant in the marine environment. It is, however, thought by many aquarists to kill parasites. Copper can have adverse effects on fish, it is not very stable in saltwater systems, it kills invertebrates, and its fate in the aquarium is not fully understood. For all these reasons, there are experts who believe copper should be eliminated as a treatment of aquarium fish disease. Nonetheless, it

The number of treatments available for marine fish diseases is very limited. This is a Longhorn Cowfish.

is still widely used in the aquarium trade. I would avoid the use of copper for all the reasons just stated, unless there are absolutely no alternatives. In this case, isolate the fish in a hospital aquarium for treatment.

Antibiotics

Antibiotics are chemotherapeutic agents that seem to be the most effective way of treating some of the common aquarium diseases. When possible, fish should be treated in a hospital tank to avoid the effects of these compounds on a mature, established aquarium. Regardless, don't expect miracle cures from antibiotics because many are not fully effective against disease.

Common Aquarium Diseases

There are hundreds of possible maladies that can afflict fish. Some are specific to certain species and some can easily be transferred between species, but fortunately not all are common in the average home aquarium. In this section, I will review the most common diseases associated with marine aquarium fish. The agents of common aquarium ailments include bacteria, viruses, fungi, and parasites.

Bacterial Diseases

Fin Rot

Causes: *Aeromonas, Pseudomonas, Vibrio* bacteria

Symptoms: This is an external bacterial infection that causes erosion or rotting of the fins and the fin rays. The base of the fins usually reddens as well. In advanced stages, the disease spreads to the gills and skin, causing bleeding and ulceration.

Treatment: The occurrence of this disease is thought to reflect deteriorating water quality. Immediate steps should be taken to improve aquarium condi-tions. Remove uneaten food, do a partial water change, and change the activated carbon in your filter. Antibiotics may be effective.

Fish Tuberculosis, Wasting Disease

Cause: *Mycobacterium* bacteria

Symptoms: There are often no external signs of this disease. A fish that seems out-wardly healthy may be internally infected. Fish that are infected may live a year or more before succumbing. Skin lesions, emaciation, labored breathing, scale loss, frayed fins, and loss of appetite are all clinical signs of this disease. Unfortunately, by the time they are manifested, it is probably too late to save the fish.

ld always be smooth and free from spots and blemishes, like this Reticulated

Treatment: These bacteria are transmitted orally through raw infected fish flesh, detritus, and the feces of infected fish. The bacteria can also infect skin wounds and lesions. The best treatment is prevention; avoid feeding raw fish and shellfish to your aquarium occupants. Antibiotics have shown some promise against these bacteria if the disease is diagnosed early. If the aquarium is heavily infected, it must be sterilized and the water discarded.

Vibriosis, Ulcer Disease

Cause: *Vibrio* bacteria

Symptoms: There are several symptoms associated with this disease, depending on the species of *Vibrio* and the species of fish. Symptoms include lethargy; darkening of color; anemia; ulcers on the skin and lower jaw; bleeding from the gills, skin, and intestinal tract; clouded eyes; loose scales; pale gills; and sudden death.

Treatment: These bacteria commonly inhabit the intestinal tract of healthy fish. They only become dangerous when stress allows infection. Poor water quality, crowding, excessive handling, and copper treatments are common causes of stress in aquarium fish. Immersion treatments with antibiotic compounds have met with some success.

Viral Diseases

Cauliflower Disease, Lymphocystis

Cause: *Cystivirus* virus

Symptoms: The main sign is fin and body lesions that are raised, whitish, warty, and have a lumpy texture like cauliflower. These lesions may take three to four weeks to reach their full size. Diseased fish typically show few signs of distress and continue to eat and behave normally. The infection is generally not fatal, but it can be transmitted to other fish in the tank.

Treatment: There is no effective treatment for this viral infection, other than to isolate the fish immediately and let the fish's immune system deal with it. This can take up to several months.

Fungal Diseases

Ichthyophonus Disease, Whirling Disease

Cause: *Ichthyphonus* fungus

Symptoms: These fungi invade the internal organs of the fish, infecting the kidney, heart, spleen, and liver. Clinical signs include emaciation, spinal curvature, darkening or paleness of the skin, roughening of the skin, fin erosion, and skin ulcers. Erratic swimming behavior can be a sign, as well. Necropsy reveals white nodules on the internal organs.

Treatment: This fungus is a parasitic organism with a complex life cycle. The fungal cysts are usually ingested by the fish, after which they burst, entering the bloodstream and infecting internal organs. Typically, fish with this disease will die up to two months after infestation. Treatment is very difficult due to the internal nature of this disease. The infected fish should be immediately removed from the aquarium to prevent other fish from becoming infected.

Exophiala Disease

Cause: *Exophiala* fungus

Symptoms: Lethargy, disorientation, and abnormal swimming are signs of this fungal infection.

Treatment: This is a poorly understood fungus and no treatment is known. You should isolate the fish to prevent other fish in the aquarium from contracting the disease.

Parasitic Diseases

Marine Velvet Disease

Cause: *Amyloodinium ocellatum* dinoflagellate protozoan

Symptoms: The gills are usually the first site of the infection. It then spreads to the skin, making it dull, patchy, and velvet-like; white spots are visible on sections of intact skin. As the disease progresses, the fish's behavior may include fasting, gasping, scratching against objects, and sluggishness. Lesions caused by the dinoflagellate can lead to secondary bacterial infection.

Treatment: This organism has three stages to its life cycle; one of them is parasitic. No completely effective treatment is known, although some antibiotics are effective. A freshwater dip sometimes dislodges these parasites from the host, but it does not kill them. Treatments are often prolonged, and the entire tank must be treated to fully eradicate the infestation.

Marine White Spot, Cryptocaryoniasis, Marine Ich

Cause: *Cryptocaryon irritans* ciliate protozoan

Symptoms: Early signs include fasting, cloudy eyes, troubled breathing, excess skin mucus, and pale skin. White spots then appear on the skin, gills, and eyes. Death follows within a few days, likely due to gill damage.

Treatment: The white spot organism can be very difficult to control. Like marine velvet, the encysted stage of this parasite is resistant to most treatments and remains in the gravel of the aquarium. A freshwater dip may be effective in killing the parasites on the fish, but does little to treat the aquarium. Copper products and antibiotics seem to have limited effectiveness.

Uronema

Cause: *Uronema marinum* ciliate protozoan
Symptoms: External ulcers, muscle and skin bleeding, lethargic behavior, sloughing of the skin, and internal infection are signs of this disease. Death may be rapid due to impaired circulation in the gills.
Treatment: Little is known about this parasite and there is no known treatment.

Tang Turbellarian Disease, Black Spot

Cause: *Paravortex* flatworms
Symptoms: Although the name implies that only Tangs are infected, this is not the case. Many species of fish can be infected by this flatworm. In the parasitic phase, these organisms look like numerous dark spots distributed unevenly over the fins, gills, and body of the fish. Other signs include fasting, listlessness, pale or whitish skin, and scratching against objects. Secondary bacterial infections can occur, as well. These signs are also common to other infestations by flatworms.

Tangs like this Powder-Blue variety are not the only fishes that can get black spot.

Treatment: Flatworms are in a phylum of their own, *Platyhelminthes*. As with most parasitic infestations, crowding facilitates their spread to other tankmates. A freshwater dip and antibiotic immersion may be effective.

Trematode Infestations

Cause: Monogenetic trematode worms
Symptoms: Many species of these worms are too small to see without a microscope. They normally infect the gills, eyes, skin, mouth, and anal opening. Infected fish usually rub themselves against objects in the aquarium trying to dislodge these parasites, which often causes skin damage that leads to secondary bacterial infections.
Treatment: These infestations are difficult to eradicate because the life cycle of these animals is poorly understood. Immersion in fresh water and antibiotics has been effective against trematodes.

Crustacean Infestations

Causes: Copepod, isopod, and argulid crustaceans
Symptoms: Most of these tiny crab-like organisms are visible to the naked eye. Copepods remain fixed in the same position, while argulids move about the surface of the host. Both groups feed by piercing the host, causing tissue damage. Fish with heavy infestations swim erratically, rub against objects, and jump. Bacteria will infect resulting lesions.
Treatment: Immediately remove fish that are infested with these parasites. Also remove aquarium decorations and either dry them to kill egg masses or immerse them in a 2 percent bleach solution for two hours. Treat infested fish by immersing them in antibiotic baths.

Other Health Problems

Head and Lateral Line Erosion

Causes: Poor water quality, nutrient deficiency, parasites
Symptoms: As in the disease of freshwater fish, hole-in-the-head, holes develop and enlarge in the sensory pits of the head and down the lateral line on the body. The disease progresses slowly, but the fish does not seem to behave differently. Advanced stages can lead to secondary bacterial infection and death.
Treatment: There are no specific treatments for this disease, although some experts recommend the use of antibiotics. Check your water quality and make any necessary adjustments. You should also make sure that you are meeting the nutritional needs of your fish. Diversify their diet and add vitamin supplements to their food.

A build-up of chemicals in your water can kill all your fish. This is a Randall's Prawn Goby.

Poisoning

Causes: Multiple causes include build-up of nitrogenous compounds (ammonia, nitrite), household chemicals (smoke, cleaners, fumes), and tap water constituents (heavy metals, chloramine)

Symptoms: Low levels of toxins in the aquarium stress fish, thereby lowering their resistance to other diseases. Higher levels cause abnormal behavior, including darting movements, jumping, and gasping at the surface.

Treatment: Make sure activated carbon is used to remove toxins and conduct a 20 to 40 percent water change. If pollutant levels are high, move the fish to the hospital tank until the main aquarium water problems are corrected.

Appendix

Learning More About Your Saltwater Aquarium

Home aquarists number in the millions throughout the world. As you become more involved in aquarium keeping, you will be surprised at how many people share this exciting hobby. When I was growing up, many of my friends had aquariums and we would spend hours working with the tank and its occupants. Later, I found myself going to my local aquarium dealer just to see new fish arrivals, talk about aquarium problems, and exchange ideas with fellow aquarists. I have picked up some of the most valuable information on fishkeeping from amateurs who enjoy the thrills of this hobby.

Clubs

In many areas, aquarium enthusiasts have formed clubs and associations where ideas and techniques are endlessly bantered about. You can find out about these organizations by asking your local aquarium supply dealer. Not only are these kinds of groups great for gathering information, but you may also find used equipment and healthy homebred fish.

Books

Thousands of books have been published on every facet of aquarium keeping. Books have been written to address virtually every aspect of the hobby. They cover broad topics like selecting fishes and very specialized topics like building a reef tank. If you have any question about aquarium keeping, the answer is likely in a book.

The book list here is just a sample of what's available for the new and experienced aquarist. Each one of the books listed has its own bibliography, which will help you delve further into the field.

Bailey, M., and G. Sandford, *The Ultimate Aquarium*, Smithmark Publishers, 1995.

Bower, C. E., *The Basic Marine Aquarium*, Charles C. Thomas Publishing, 1983.

Burgess, W. E., *Marine Aquariums: A Complete Introduction*, TFH Publications, 1989.

Burgess, W. E., H. R. Axelrod, and R. E. Hunziker III, *Atlas of Marine Aquarium Fishes*, TFH Publications, 1990.

Dakin, N., *The Macmillan Book of the Marine Aquarium*, Macmillan Publishing Co., 1992.

Delbeek, C. J., and J. Sprung, *The Reef Aquarium: A Comprehensive Guide to the Identification and Care of Tropical Marine Invertebrates*, Vol. I, Ricordea Publishing, 1994.

DeVito, C., and G. Skomal, *The Everything Tropical Fish Book*, Adams Media Corp., 2000.

Eschmeyer, W. M., *Catalogue of the Genera of Recent Fishes*, California Academy of Sciences, 1990.

Fenner, R. M., *The Conscientious Marine Aquarist*, Microcosm Ltd., 1998.

Gratzek, J. B., *Aquariology: Fish Diseases and Water Chemistry*, Tetra Press, 1992.

Helfman, G. S., B. B. Collette, and D. E. Facey, *The Diversity of Fishes*, Blackwell Science, 1999.

Kay, G., *The Tropical Marine Fish Survival Manual*, Quarto, 1995.

Lundegaard, G., *Keeping Marine Fish: An Aquarium Guide*, Sterling Publishing Co., 1991.

Melzak, M., *The Marine Aquarium Manual,* Arco Publishing, 1984.

Michael, S. W., *Reef Fishes, Volume 1: A Guide to Their Identification*, Microcosm, 1998.

Michael, S.W., *PocketExpert Guide Series for Aquarists and Underwater Naturalists, Marine Fishes: 500+ Essential-to-Know Aquarium Species*, TFH Publications, 1999.

Mills, D., *Aquarium Fish*, Dorling Kindersley Publishing, 1993.

Moyle, P. B., and J. J. Cech, Jr., *Fishes: An Introduction to Ichthyology*, Prentice-Hall, 1982.

Sandford, G., *An Illustrated Encyclopedia of Aquarium Fish*, Howell Book House, 1995.

Scott, P. W., *The Complete Aquarium*, Dorling Kindersley Publishing, 1995.

Shimek, R., *The Coral Reef Aquarium: An Owner's Guide to a Happy Healthy Pet*, Howell Book House, 1999.

Shimek, R. *A PocketExpert Guide to Marine Invertebrates: 500+ Essential-to-Know Aquarium Species*, Microcosm, 2005.

Skomal, G. B., *Saltwater Aquariums For Dummies*, John Wiley and Sons, 2002.

Skomal, G. B., *Clownfishes in the Aquarium*, TFH Publications, 2004.

Spotte, S., *Seawater Aquariums*, John Wiley and Sons, 1979.

Spotte, S., *Captive Seawater Fishes: Science and Technology*, John Wiley and Sons, 1992.

Sprung, J., and C. J. Delbeek, *The Reef Aquarium: A Comprehensive Guide to the Identification and Care of Tropical Marine Invertebrates*, Vol. II, Ricordea Publishing, 1997.

Stoskopf, M. K., *Fish Medicine*, W.B. Saunders Co., 1993.

Stratton, R. F., *Aquarium Filtration*, Yearbooks, 2000.

Tullock, J. H., *Your First Marine Aquarium*, Barrons Educational Series, 1998.

Magazines

Monthly aquarium magazines provide you with some of the most up-to-date information on aquarium keeping. Timely articles on breeding, feeding, disease, and species-specific husbandry entertain and inform the new aquarist. Product information and classified advertising are excellent features of an aquarium magazine. Magazines that have proven to be very good conduits of information are:

Freshwater and Marine Aquarium
P.O. Box 487
Sierra Madre, CA 91024
(800) 523-1736
www.famamagazine.com

Practical Fishkeeping
Bretton Court
Bretton, Peterborough
PE3 8DZ, United Kingdom
www.practicalfishkeeping.co.uk/home.asp

Tropical Fish Hobbyist
One TFH Plaza
Neptune City, NJ 07753
(908) 988-8400
www.tfh.com

Internet

The amount of aquarium information on the Internet is unbelievable. It seems to be the place where people gather to exchange information about the hobby. This is by far the fastest way to obtain and exchange information on aquarium keeping. If you have access to the Internet, then you have unlimited access to a vast amount of information on this hobby. Internet resources include chat groups, equipment, photos, links, husbandry information, classified ads, events, and on and on and on.

There are Internet networks for fish enthusiasts that you can join. This gives you access to hobbyists, professional aquarists, researchers, breeders, and vendors of aquarium products. You can even get immediate advice from staff about sick fish.

There is so much on the Internet that you will quickly be overwhelmed by all the sites. Many experts, vendors, and amateurs have web pages as well. Any good search engine will help you access these resources, but here a few that I like.

Aquaria Central
www.aquariacentral.com
Articles, chat rooms, message boards, and species profiles complement this big shopping site.

Aqua Link
www.aqualink.com
A huge supplier of aquarium supplies; plus the site also has articles, message boards, and links to many fishkeeping communities.

Aquarium Fish.com
www.aquariumfish.com
The web site of *Aquarium Fish* magazine includes article archives, a forum, classified ads, and species profiles.

Aquarium Global Resource
www.aquariuminstruments.com
You will find every type of aquarium equipment and instrumentation on this site.

Aquarium.net
www.aquarium.net
This site is a compendium of other shopping sites, sorted into saltwater, reef, marine, and other categories.

Aquatic Book Shop

www.seahorses.com

Offers a very large selection of new and used books, magazines, and videos on fishing, aquariums, and ichthyology, for hobbyists at all levels.

Fish Base

www.fishbase.org

Search for information on any fish species by using a wide range of criteria, including scientific name, common name, native country, and fish family. You'll also find articles on biodiversity and behavior, and a glossary.

Fish Index

www.fishindex.com

You'll find species profiles, photos, videos, a glossary, message boards, a chat room, and conversion calculators.

Index